THE

*The T*

### WILLIAM K. MCDONOUGH

The St. Paul Center Studies in Biblical Theology and Spirituality
### SCOTT HAHN, GENERAL EDITOR

PUBLISHED BY ST. ANTHONY MESSENGER PRESS
CINCINNATI, OHIO

*Nihil obstat:*   John A. Goodwine
                  Censor Librorum

*Imprimatur:*     +Francis Cardinal Spellman
                  Archbishop of New York
                  October 4, 1962

The *nihil obstat* and *imprimatur* are official declarations that a book or pamphlet is free of doctrinal or moral error. No implication is contained therein that those who have granted the *nihil obstat* and *imprimatur* agree with the contents, opinions or statements expressed.

Scripture citations are taken from the Challoner revision of the Douay-Rheims Bible.

Cover design by Michael J. Frazier
Book design by Phillips Robinette, O.F.M.

ISBN 0-86716-711-4

First edition published by The Macmillan Company in 1963.

Library of Congress catalogue card number: 63-9235

Published by Servant Books, an imprint of St. Anthony Messenger Press.

St. Anthony Messenger Press
28 W. Liberty Street
Cincinnati, OH 45202
www.AmericanCatholic.org

Printed in the United States of America.
Printed on acid-free paper.

05 06 07 08 09 10 5 4 3 2 1

To
Our Lady
Fairest Daughter of the Father
Maiden Mother of the Son
Radiant Bride of the Holy Spirit

# *CONTENTS*

*Scott Hahn, General Editor*

The St. Paul Center Studies in Biblical Theology and
Spirituality are a series of books designed to help
Christians in their study of the Word of God. Dr. Scott
Hahn serves as general editor, and the St. Paul Center
for Biblical Theology, founded by Dr. Hahn, cosponsors
the series with Servant Books.

Each volume helps to fulfill the mission of the St. Paul
Center, which is to promote life-transforming study of
Scripture in the Catholic tradition. The Center serves
clergy and laity, students and scholars, with a variety of
research and study tools, from books and publications to
multimedia programs and a fully stocked Web library. All
efforts promote an integrated study of the Word of God:
the Old Testament and the New, the Bible within the
liturgy; Scripture illumined by the tradition and the
Magisterium.

We believe that every generation of disciples should
know Jesus in the breaking of the bread (see Luke
24:13–37) and exclaim, as his first-generation disciples
did: "Did not our hearts burn within us while he talked
to us on the road, while he opened to us the Scriptures?"

# FOREWORD

Father William K. McDonough (1900-1982) was, in many ways, an ordinary parish priest. He served as an assistant and then as a pastor, in both city and country parishes. In fifty-five years of ministry, he found his daily strength in "Breviary, Rosary, Mass, and his love for the sacrament of reconciliation."[1]

What set Father McDonough apart was not the circumstances of his Christian life but the reflection and insight he gained from living it. These he distilled in crystalline clarity and simplicity in his one and only book, the book you hold in your hands, *The Divine Family: The Trinity and Our Life in God*.

Father McDonough was a man steeped in the biblical and liturgical movements that bloomed in the first half of the twentieth century and found their full flower in the Second Vatican Council. Those two movements were one for him, as they were for the council fathers. His meditation on the Scriptures was his preparation for Mass; his celebration of Mass illuminated his reading of the Bible. "He anticipated the readings of the day," recalled a close priest-friend, "and also the prayers of celebration. The introductory public rite was the conclusion of his own reflective preparation. When he began he was disposed and undistracted."[2] We readers, who never knew him, sense that concentration in the pages of *The Divine Family.* Here, Father McDonough produced a profound work of biblical theology, drawn from the whole Bible but especially from the teachings of Saint John and Saint Paul, and especially from their interpretation of the Old Testament. For the inspired authors were the first theologians, and their milieu was that of their ancestors in Israel, the chosen people. Like their ancestors, they defined their world by a single concept. The Jewish scholar Alan Segal has put it starkly: "The root metaphor underlying Hebrew society is expressed in the word *covenant.*"[3] For the biblical authors, covenant is the quality most characteristic of God's dealings with mankind. Covenant is the trademark of God, evident at every stage of history. From Adam, Noah, and Abraham to Moses and David

That, however, raises the question: What exactly is a covenant? Frank Moore Cross of Harvard describes covenant as the "legal means by which the duties and privileges of kinship may be extended to another individual or group, including aliens."[4] Covenant is what established, defined, and renewed the family bond. Marriage was a covenant, as was adoption. But even international treaties took the form of covenants, expressing a new diplomatic relationship in terms of kinship. So it was always somewhat curious that Israel spoke of its relationship with God in terms of covenant. That seemed to imply kinship with God, an astonishing and seemingly improbable thing.

When we move forward in the biblical canon, we see that what is implicit in the Old suddenly explodes as infinitely explicit in the New. The root metaphor develops—from covenant to family. Consider just the language of God's fatherhood. In chapters 5-7 of Matthew's Gospel, we find seventeen references to God's fatherhood—more than in the entire Old Testament combined! And that doesn't even begin to consider the Gospel's usage of other family terms: brother, sister, mother, family, home, table, and so on.

Contemplation of the Word of God taught Father McDonough that not all metaphors are created equal. God's fatherhood is His proper name. Father is the proper name of the first person of the Blessed Trinity, and it is the proper name not only because it is a noun but also because it is a verb. Father is who God is, and *father* is what God is eternally doing. That is why there is a Son who is coeternal, not smaller and younger. As the root metaphor of Hebrew culture was covenant, so the root metaphor of Christianity is family. In the New Testament, the language of covenant recedes and the language of kinship pervades.

*The Divine Family* appeared in 1963, anticipating the teaching of the Second Vatican Council—and, even more, its interpretation and development by Pope John Paul II. It was he who wrote: "God in His deepest mystery is not a solitude, but a family, since He has in Himself fatherhood, sonship, and the essence of the family, which is love."[5]

There is no more astonishing fact than this: that God is a family and He has made us His children, sons and daughters in His eternal Son!

This is the truth that Father McDonough learned from the Scriptures, from the Church Fathers and the saints, and from the great theologians of the Catholic tradition. I am especially pleased by his attention to Matthias Joseph Scheeben, an important thinker who has too long been neglected. Father McDonough knew "the divine family," and he communicated it in everything he wrote and said and did. Those who knew him say he exuded peace. His brother priests called him "Gentle Willie," and his eulogist noted that Father McDonough "made little noise" as he went about his work. I have never seen an unsmiling photograph of the man.

He died in 1982 on "the day he cherished above all the others in the Church's calendar"[6]—Holy Thursday, when the Church celebrates the institution of the New Covenant priesthood.

*Scott Hahn, Ph.D.*
*General Editor*

## *Notes*

1.      "Obituary: Father McDonough Dies on Holy Thursday," *The Church World*, Portland, Maine, April 15, 1982, p. 10.

2.      *Ibid.*

3.      Alan Segal. *Rebecca's Children: Judaism and Christianity in the Roman World* (Cambridge, Mass.: Harvard University Press, 1986), p. 4.

4.      F. M. Cross, "Kinship and Covenant in Ancient Israel," in *From Epic to Canon: History and Literature in Ancient Israel* (Baltimore: Johns Hopkins University Press, 1998), p. 8.

5.      Pope John Paul II, *Puebla: A Pilgrimage of Faith* (Boston: Daughters of St. Paul, 1979), p. 86. See also *Letter to Families* (Boston: St. Paul Books & Media, 1994), p. 14 and *Catechism of the Catholic Church*, # 2845.

6.      "Obituary," p. 10.

# *PREFACE*

The dogma of the Most Blessed Trinity is the fundamental doctrine of our faith. It is the most sublime mystery of revelation; the mystery of mysteries. Yet with all its significance, we could well call it the "forgotten mystery."

True, we profess our faith in one God in three Divine Persons. But is there not a sort of silent implication, sometimes even expressed, that this is really something too deep to penetrate; something outside the pale of the practical or personal; to be kept at a reverent distance?

It does, of course, receive a passing recognition in the habitual sign of the cross. Yet how often is this no more than a token gesture, made casually, without reflection, as a perfunctory habit?

Then, again, when we really pray, even fervently, almost always we address Christ, as our only Lord. But did He not reveal His intimacy with the other Two—His Father, His Comfortor? Why? Precisely to acquaint us with Them, in the hope that acquaintance would grow to intimacy for us; that we would let Him lead us closer into the bosom of the Father, in the fellowship of Their mutual Spirit of Love.

Finally, the entire content of His revelation begs an understanding of this first and greatest of His secrets. It is the core that holds together, as it unfolds in petal fashion, all the related aspects of His message.

In other words, Christ intended us to know this mystery "in depth," proportioned to our capacity, in the here and now. He named Names, to be remembered; to be called upon; to be lived with, in exciting anticipation, till the day dawns when He will reveal clearer "depth" in vision—when we shall see Them, face to face.

It is the humble hope that this little book will help to open, somewhat, the shape of a mystery too often kept tightly closed inside, in the bud, for fear of getting lost in the deep.

# ACKNOWLEDGMENTS

Among the rewarding features of writing this book has been the sustained interest of many friends. It gives me great pleasure to acknowledge my gratitude to them all. In particular, I must mention the following:

I express my sincerest appreciation to the Very Rev. Reginald Redlon, O.F.M., Superior of the Franciscan House of Studies, Rye Beach, N.H., for encouraging me from the beginning, and for the cordial hospitality he and his entire community extended me as a welcome to Rye Beach, where I wrote part of this book.

I especially thank the Rev. John Walsh, S.J., Dean of the Theology Faculty of Weston College, for carefully reading the entire text and for suggesting several revisions for clarity of expression.

I acknowledge my debt of gratitude to Miss Catherine M. Neale of New York City for all her gracious assistance as my literary agent and for her diligence in preparing and editing the manuscript of this book.

# ONE

# Divine Spirit

When the greatest sculptor of all time, Michelangelo, finished his masterpiece of Moses, he struck it (they say), giving it a command: "Speak!" When you gaze on this magnificent work of art, the command does not surprise you, so lifelike is it. The very beard of Moses seems to tremble with his anger at the Chosen People for falling into idolatry, which anger is the mood of the subject of the statue. But, of course, the statue did not obey the artist's command. How could it? For all its majestic vitality, it had no real life. It was, after all, only cold, lifeless marble.

When the same Michelangelo received a commission to paint some pictures on the ceiling of the Vatican's Sistine Chapel, he said, "I am no painter." He was wrong. His genius in painting equaled his genius in sculpture. And in his "moving pictures" on this ceiling he outdid himself. It was his cadenza, and executed literally while on the flat of his back.

Without doubt, the *pièce de resistance* in this living panorama is his depiction of the creation of Adam and Eve. So masterful is it that it happens to be the nearest "picturing" of a spirit that we have. It is a painting, but the subject appears to be the work of the Divine Sculptor Who succeeded in doing what the great human sculptor could not do: make a statue "speak."

> The whole ceiling is a display of total mastery over the human body as an instrument of expression for the soul, but the creation of Adam stands for all time as the supreme expression of the spirit manifesting itself in flesh.... The limp yet latently powerful figure of our first parent reclines on earth. The fingers of God and man almost touch and the gift of life leaps the gap like an electric current.[1]

This was, of course, an artist's conception of the creation of the first human soul. He was not concerned with the "time element," nor with the historical physical condition of the material that would constitute the first human body at the moment of its fusion with spirit. His concept was the fusion and its immediate consequence: life. He wanted to show what really made Adam a masterpiece —the jewel within the casket, spirit.

> In looking at His creation of Eve we see that

> The Lord is standing up on the right, wrapped in the folds of a great mantle. Before Him lies the sleeping Adam. His young body seems to

emanate from God, and lift itself against the trunk of a tree. This interrupted movement is resumed by Eve who rises slowly from his side, her hands folded in prayer and her astonished gaze fixed upon the Creator towards Whom she leans in mute gratitude and adoration, drawn by a gesture of the divine hand which rouses her and calls her to Himself.[2]

If Eve were merely a painting she would not know her God, or thank Him. Adam and Eve of Paradise, then, could do what the Moses of Michelangelo could not do, precisely because they had received, within, the spirit of life.

It is important to think about the human spirit because "God is spirit" (John 4:24), according to St. John's perfect description. And right here we must make a point very clear. We are not becoming anthropomorphic—a cumbersome term invented by theologians to warn us of the danger of endowing God with all kinds of human qualities. No, we are not bringing God down to our level, but are merely observing how our spiritual natures act, in order to get some kind of a lever to try to rise as high as we can to God's level. We have to start someplace; so we start with ourselves. For our souls are spirits. This should not surprise us, because we are "made to the image and likeness of God." The likeness consists especially in our having a spirit. The only other creatures enjoying this same priceless gift are the angels.

Basically all three kinds of spirits, human, angelic, and divine, act in somewhat similar fashion.

That is to say, the essential activity of all spirits is to know and to love (endowed, as the catechism puts it, with understanding and free will).

The greatest difficulty about the spiritual is, of course, that we cannot *see* it. Therefore it does not seem to interest us very much. Why bother? But since we have to have pictures to understand anything, it seems—and while few people see the Sistine Chapel—we do have other ways of "picturing" spirits, at least getting a kind of picture. We might call it an "action picture," seeing how a spirit acts, in addition to its animation of the body so that tongue, eyes, hands, limbs respond to it.

Consider, for instance, a group of people planning a picnic. Everybody does a lot of talking. The plans just grow and grow with every new suggestion of what to do, where to go, who goes, how to get there and, last but not least, what to eat. Now nobody would ever say that these several physical bodies present made all these exciting plans. For the picnic-idea to grow, there had to be the thought conveyed through sounds made by vocal cords, as they vibrated through ether waves and registered in eardrums. There had to be "thought length" (broadcasted and received by something other than the body) as well as wavelength—or else no picnic. If any little dogs were present all they heard were so many noises and they could not make one contribution.

So we have to admit that, since all these human beings planned a picnic, they must have had some inner power that enabled them to understand the picnic-idea and that could contribute many other interesting ideas as to how to make it an exciting affair. Otherwise there just would never be any picnic. From the way the participants acted in arranging and enjoying the picnic we have to say that an invisible power made it possible for them to "know" the meaning of picnic. If we say they were, at the moment, very "picnic-minded," they must have had minds in addition to bodies. And behind every human action there must be some kind of "knowing" process (hard as it may be, sometimes, to see any sense in it).

Now the only other way people act, because of this inner force we call spirit, is to choose what the mind recognizes as appealing. This we call "love." Though it is a very loose use of the word, we could say that some people dearly love picnics. They choose freely this idea of how to have fun, in preference to many others. There is something about picnics that for them is irresistible. So their hearts reach out to picnics.

Fortunately there are higher grades of love. On the human level, there is the supreme example of a mother's love for her child, and the child's love for his mother. How does she act? Once she knows God has given her this tiny bundle of squirming humanity, she clutches it, feeds it, warms it, plans for it, slaves for it, risks her life for it. But perhaps this is only biological determination: she thrills at the sight of him, loves the mere sensation of his caress. But maybe she is blind and her arms are temporarily paralyzed. Still, something within her reaches out to this child. For want of another word to explain the way she acts, mysteriously, to be sure, but factually, we say she "loves" this baby that she "knows" is hers.

Oh yes! But how does she act differently from the mother bear with her little cubs? There is the same maternal instinct in each case, you might say. True, but the bear must follow its instinct; the mother is free to suppress it. She has what the bear lacks: power of choosing. She can reject the child. Not so the bear. Again, over and above the fact that the baby is hers and immensely lovable, the mother "knows" where he ultimately came from and whither is his destiny (with her). This intensifies her natural love. The bear has no ideas whatsoever, and only blind, brute, maternal instinct. Quite a difference!

Another way to determine the spiritual is to contrast it with the material. Spiritual is the opposite of material. A material creature is made up of parts: the human body with its head, hands, feet, etc. All of these can be divided, cut off, and destroyed. They are forever undergoing a change. A spirit, on the other hand, is essentially simple, having no parts. Since it cannot break down into parts, for it has no parts, a spirit of itself is immortal. It needs no space; space is a necessity only for matter. That is why the soul is not confined to one part, or to several parts, of the body. It animates the entire body with all its various parts. Moreover, since it is simple and cannot be divided, a man's soul suffers no loss when he accidentally loses a finger in operating a handsaw. The finger in ceasing to be part of the body no longer has life because it is separated from the man's spirit. It is dead as soon as it is severed from the rest of the living body, every part of which continues to be animated by the soul.

But, again, we must not think of the soul as taking up any space in the body. A spirit cannot occupy space. Space is "emptiness" waiting for something material to fill it, such as an airplane in the sky. Think, too, of all the space needed in an antique shop! We are so continually occupied with things that require space that it is hard to think of any reality not being in space. But if the soul were present in the body, as a material reality occupying space, then the surgeon could discover it, as he does your appendix. Perhaps the best way to convince ourselves that spirits cannot occupy space, is to remember that nobody would ever think of trying to capture the soul of a dying man in order to put it into another body whose soul has already departed. When we think of spirit as "life," this becomes all the clearer. We never think of dissecting life (as we do the lifeless body); we never think of moving life from one space to another.

When we approach the Spirit of God, after thinking about our own spirit life, we are ascending to a vastly higher level. This we must always keep well in mind. And while we try to avoid thinking about God as we think of human beings, nevertheless we are bound to make use of analogies or similes. These will be inadequate but will help us toward understanding, just as a crutch enables us to walk.

We said that there are three kinds of spirits. There are human spirits, angelic spirits, and *the* (not a) Divine Spirit; several human souls and angels—only *one*

Divine Spirit. It was easy enough to put "life" into the meaning of the human spirit after seeing it at work as the life-giving force of the body, and seeing it also as knowing and loving. But calling God as spirit seems vague and nebulous. There is something ghostly about the word as we ordinarily use it. Holy Ghost, as the name of the Third Person of the Holy Trinity, confirms our impression of ghostliness. It is Old English and we do much better today using the name Holy Spirit. When once we learn the root meaning of spirit it becomes descriptive of God. This word is derived from the Latin *spirare*, meaning "to breathe". Now nothing, absolutely nothing, is so indicative of life as breathing. Do we not say a man is dead when he has stopped breathing? From this meaning the Latin *spiritus* has come to signify life. So by calling God Spirit, He becomes very real and alive for us. There is nothing so alive as *life*. Remember that in the creation of Adam it is God (Spirit-Life, source of all life) Who "breathed" into Adam's face the breath of life, and man became a living soul (spirit, like God).

Now *Divine* is the best adjective we can use with Spirit, referring to God. Sometimes we hear God spoken of as the Infinite Spirit. But *infinite* is too indefinite. In fact, in mathematics we use this term to express an indefinite degree. Then, again, *infinite* is negative. It means nonlimited. God's "qualities" are unlimited, and here as an attribute of God infinite has a definite meaning. Sometimes we call God the Supreme Being. *Supreme* is terribly up in the clouds. It also sounds too much like "super," and there is danger of thinking of God as superman. To refer to God as a *being* is not very distinctive either. Remember, everything in the entire gamut of creation is a being, from angels to microbes. But when we say God is divine, this means something to us. Only *One* is divine. The very word has a ring to it. *Divine* is positive. We never refer to the infinite nature of Christ, nor to His supreme nature, but to His divine nature.

This emphasis on the divine is important because it comes back again and again in the entire content of the key mysteries of Christianity (especially in interplay with the human). Christ came primarily to incorporate us into His divine life. We become divine, that is, Godlike. Again, *divine* is almost concrete; *infinite* is very abstract. Nothing is as concrete as God. Too often do men think of Him as the vaguest of abstractions. We must take God out of the abstract and see Him as real, real to us. Calling God the Divine Spirit helps us to do this.

In trying to understand the human spirit we examined how it "works" and saw how it animates, knows, and loves. This was looking at the nature of the soul. A nature is that which makes a thing what it is, causing it to act the way it does. It is of the very nature of a bird to fly, a dog to bark, a brook to flow, a man to know and love. And since, as already mentioned, God is a Spirit, it must be His nature (in common with all spirits) to know and love. His nature is the one divine nature. The staggering difference between this and all other natures is beyond the beyond, exhausting all superlatives. The divine nature has all perfections in an infinite degree.

One of the perfections of God which should really fascinate us, though it more often mystifies us, is His eternity. We cannot say there never was a "time" when God did not exist, because with God there is no time. God exists (knows, loves, acts) in the ever-present "now," without beginning or end. We sometimes get the impression that God did not "do much" before He made a world. "However did He occupy Himself?" we ask. This wonder is prompted by the fact that the world is tremendously impressive with its grandeur, magnitude, unfathomed resources, breathtaking beauty, and lately with what scientists have discovered of its antiquity in millions of years, and we can think of nothing over and beyond all this. True, it is an overwhelming proof of the existence and infinite power of the God Who alone could have made it; but we forget that despite its significance this world is really only a "pastime," a sort of "sideline" with God. Keeping it in existence, poised as it were at the tip of His finger, is not His sole "occupation." He is "busy" outside the realm of time, in the depths of the eternal.

This is not to say that we do not matter much to Him. On the contrary, it should be consoling to us that before time dawned God thought of each one of us, planned to make us, loved the very "thought" of us. We have really existed, so to speak, for all eternity in the mind of God. Though we have something much more tremendous to say about how God occupied Himself before He made the world, it is rewarding (if surprising) to know how long He has loved us. This mysterious eternity of the divine nature shows another vast difference between the eternal God and ourselves, who are limited by time; it makes God, however, all the more marvelous to contemplate.

We could, of course, examine what to us appear as various perfections of the divine nature, dividing mentally what is indivisible in God. But we say everything when we say that God is a symphony of every possible perfection. He is ultimate perfection, the ultimate of ultimates, divinely blended. Now it becomes supremely important for us to get back to that very interesting and provocative question: What did God do before He had the world on His hands? Here we see something of the real grandeur of the divine nature.

Recalling what we have already observed of a spirit's basic nature to know and love gives us a lead. But we must first take another look at the nature of puny little man. Take a great man, any one you will—say, Michelangelo. We do not get the real measure of this genius merely from his immortal masterpieces. Far from it. It is sad but true that many a genius is a pitiful weakling as a man, despite the greatness of his works. Not so the decorator of the Sistine Chapel. Fortunately he left some notes. Among these we read: "It is not enough for a painter to be a great and accomplished master-craftsman. I firmly believe that his life should be pure and holy, so far as possible, so that the Holy Spirit may guide his thoughts. ...Beautiful painting is a shadow from the brush of God. It is music. It is melody. Very lofty intelligence alone can grasp it."

Herein, revealed in his thoughts, lies the real greatness of the man. And the point of all this is that interior activity is greater than exterior. In other words, if the human mind could not contain ideas, human hands could never build a house, paint a picture, drive a car, play a game of golf.

Take the case of a lesser celebrity, someone in the public eye, who has achieved notable success in any field. How the reporters love to get an interview! How we love to read the profile, in order to learn what goes on inside this person's mind, apart from interest in his accomplishments that are known so well! We want to know what his purposes, dreams, obstacles, hardships, and sympathies are. Then we get to know the man, aside from what he has done. His work will become dated; the man is immortal. This fact makes him vastly more interesting. That is why autobiography tops biography. It tells secrets otherwise hidden.

Now if the interior life of a man is so much more exciting than his outer activities, what about God? When we said that the Divine Spirit is life and therefore active, we tried to eliminate the vagueness often associated with the word "spirit." Now we have to see that divine activity does not consist merely in the making of a world. We see, also, that God did not make a world because He was lonely, all by Himself. No, because just as in the case of the human spirit, there are in the Divine Spirit two kinds of activity: interior and exterior. And by the same token, the interior life of God is tremendously more vital and fascinating than His creation of this little world, in which we see His exterior activity.

We read in the Scriptures: "The heavens shew forth the glory of God, and the firmament declareth the work of his hands" (Psalms 18:2). And again: "By the word of the Lord the heavens were established; and all the power of them by the spirit of his mouth: Gathering together the waters of the sea, as in a vessel; laying up the depths in storehouses" (Psalms 32:6–7). But just as in the case of wanting to know the person behind great human accomplishments, all these marvels of creation should entice us to learn something of the life within the divine nature that has produced so much for our delight.

This we can do, even by our own efforts. In a way, we can "explore" for ourselves something of the divine mind. We already are aware of the truth that God knows and loves. Now we can get to know something more of this God Who conceived the idea of this world with its oceans, mountains, sunsets, roses, gold, homes, deer, etc., and Who loves all these things too, but loves us much more, for whom He made them. In doing this we start at our own level again.

We say of someone who is very smart yet very thoughtful: "He thinks of everything. What an active mind he has!" Then in looking down from some mountain peak at the "world that is charged with the grandeur of God," we look up and into the divine mind whence all this came. To call God's mind "active" seems such a feeble attempt at description. But such is the poverty of human speech before the divine. Our minds literally stagger

13

when we realize that all the vast multiplicity and inexhaustible variety evidenced in creation are really only samples of billions of other possible marvels God could create.

Even more alluring is the fact that all the ideas back of this symphony of creation are from within the divine mind. So the colors of this world's pageantry seem to pale in comparison with the fecundity and divine wealth that now appear within this divine nature (behind the "scenes")! How we long to know more about God, more about His inner "activity"! Then this world becomes too small to satisfy us. We see that all these divine ideas have to be "within." Before the world was made, there was nothing outside. Unlike human artists, inventors, and scientists who need material to work with, God planned this world and willed it to spring into existence out of nothing.

When we said we could discover the fact of this inner life of God, which is much more exciting than His external works, we meant just that. Such are the findings of philosophy. Since reality—things that are—necessarily includes God, the greatest reality, a philosophy which does not include our knowledge of God is a pretty thin brand (and there are such brands). We can hardly say that to seek to know God is too deep and not very practical. Hardly, when it is our main business in life to know and love God; the main reason why we have a mind.

We have been philosophizing all along so far. Rising from our own spiritual nature to a consideration of the divine nature, we have discovered that God, too, knows and loves, and that His knowledge and love are without measure. He is the font of all knowledge, the exemplar of every idea. We saw that the minds of the greatest genius, philosopher, poet, and scientist contain but the faintest reflections of the divine mind. Human ideas are as mist in comparison with those from the font that is divine.

As for ascending from human love to divine, we can only say that the love of a mother for her child, and the child's love for its mother, are as ice, compared to the burning, volcanic fire of divine love.

But the mystery of mysteries, the marvel of marvels, is that this divine knowing and loving nature is knowable and lovable, not only to itself, but to us—the wherefore of our existence and of the whole world as well.

But, of course, such findings will never satisfy us. God would still be far too remote. How frustrating if this were all, with nothing more to know! By our own efforts this is as far as we can go. We really never get to know a person by reading about him, to say nothing of getting to love him. It is one thing to read the profile of an interesting character, or to have an interview with him, and quite another thing when he invites you to dinner, to meet his family. Then you see how he lives in his complete life.

This is precisely what the burning love of God prompted Him to do for us. To compensate for our inability to know more about Him. He has condescended to tell us the marvelous "secret" about His intimate inner life;

the fact of the Divine Trinity. And this brings us to the story of the Divine Family.

The philosophical bird's-eye view that we have had helps to condition us to the divine light in which the secret stands unveiled, enabling us to behold its splendor with a little more clarity, enticing us closer to its warmth.

## Notes

1. Frank and Dorothy Getlein, *Christianity in Art* (Milwaukee: Bruce, 1959), pp. 125–126.
2. D. Redig de Campos, *Wanderings among Vatican Paintings* (G. Bardi, Rome, 1953), p. 148.

## *DIVINE SECRET*

The secret is this: God does not live a lonely life. For within His utter simplicity three divine Personalities possess the one same nature and live Their divine life in the utmost intimacy; intimacy attainable only in a family that is divine. The secret, then, is a mystery: the inner life of God consists in a perfect unity and multiplicity at the same time. We cannot know *how*; we can only know that this is true. For God told us so!

When did He reveal the secret to us here below? It was not necessary. Why not wait till we get to heaven? The only answer: Love does such things! He did not wish to wait. What real lover ever holds back secrets? This mystery is a mystery of love. Remember, "God is love" (1 John 4:8).

Where do we find this secret? We read it in the Sacred Scriptures. "The New Testament is the revelation of One God in Three Persons and of our union with him."[1] In fact it has been said that the entire New Testament is a development of the doctrine of the Divine Trinity:[2] that in one God there are three Divine Persons, really distinct; each having one and the same divine nature. In reading the New Testament we find hundreds of references to the names of the Father, Son, and Holy Spirit. And while the sacred authors do not use the words "person" and "nature" as such, they use expressions which correspond to the ideas of nature and personality for each member. For example, they describe attributes or qualities of the Father, Son, and Holy Spirit which show Them to have characteristics of real Persons acting according to Their one divine nature, that is, knowing, willing (loving), acting. For by a person we mean any individual subject existing in a rational nature to which all the subject's actions are attributed.

Thus the Father *knows*: "no one knows who the Son is except the Father" (Luke 10:22); the Son *knows*: "Christ Jesus, in whom are hidden all the treasures of wisdom and knowledge" (Colossians 2:2–3); the Holy Spirit *knows*: "the things of God no one knows but the Spirit of God" (1 Corinthians 2:11).

Each Person *wills*: "not everyone who says to me 'Lord, Lord,' shall enter the kingdom of heaven; but he who does the will of my Father in heaven" (Matthew 7:21); "no one who knows who...the Father is except the Son, and him to whom the Son chooses to reveal him" (Luke 10:22); "but all these things are the work of one and the same Spirit who allots to everyone according to his will" (1 Corinthians 12:11).

The three Divine Persons *act*: "but the Father dwelling in me, it is he who does the works" (John 14:10); "For the works which the Father has given me to accomplish, these very works that I do, bear witness to me" (John 5:36); "But all these things are the work of one and the same Spirit" (1 Corinthians 12:11).

Scripture assures us, moreover, that these three Divine Persons are *distinct* one from the other: "This is my beloved Son, in whom I am well pleased" (Matthew 3:17); "I came forth from the Father and have come into the world. Again I leave the world and go to the Father" (John 16:28); "But the Advocate, the Holy Spirit, whom the Father will send in my name, he will teach you all things" (John 14:26); "For if I do not go, the Advocate will not come to you; but if I go I will send him to you" (John 16:7).

Also we learn from the texts of Scripture that not only is each Person distinct but all possess *divine nature*, being truly God: "Father, the hour has come! Glorify thy Son, that thy Son may glorify thee,...Now this is everlasting life, that they may know thee, the only true God" (John 17:1, 3); "Have this mind in you which was also in Christ Jesus, who though he was by nature God, did not consider being equal to God a thing to be clung to, but emptied himself, taking the nature of a slave and being made like unto men" (Philippians 2:5–7); "Ananias, why has Satan tempted thy heart, that thou shouldst lie to the Holy Spirit and by fraud keep back part of the price of the land?... Thou hast not lied to men, but to God" (Acts 5:3–4).

Finally we see that each Divine Person possesses *one* and the *same* divine nature—three Persons in one God: "Is God the God of the Jews only and not of the Gentiles also? Indeed of the Gentiles also. ...For there is but one God" (Romans 3:29–30); "For there are three that bear witness in heaven: the Father, the Word and the Holy Spirit; and these three are one" (1 John 5:7).

The secret is all there—written simply, clearly, as it came from the lips of Christ and was taught by Him to His disciples. Before He told it, it was a secret. Once revealed, it was secret no longer. He wanted it told and retold till the end of time. And that is precisely what has happened. The apostles, through the inspiration of God, not only inscribed it in the pages of the New Testament, but also, as preachers of Christ's word, they taught it to their followers; their successors continued to teach it uninterruptedly.

This continual teaching of all the truths of Christianity is called oral Tradition, the handing down of the official teaching of Christ through the Catholic Church from one generation to the next. This consists in no mere haphazard passing on of beliefs like legends, in the human tradition, that can easily become distorted and lose their original meaning. This oral Tradition of the Church is divine, as divine as Scripture, and serves, along with Scripture, as the source of all the truths revealed by Christ. From our catechism we recall that the indwelling of the Holy Spirit in the Church enables her to *teach*, sanctify, and rule all her members; teaching them infallibly. The Church exercises this divine role of teaching and interpreting all that Christ revealed by drawing from Scripture and Tradition. Her voice is the living voice of her Founder, keeping alive the heritage of His Gospel, both in its written and its oral content.

Tradition is not only a turning to the teaching of the past, but is also a present, living, developing teaching of everything revealed directly by Christ or through the apostles until their death. The Church uses many means of exercising her teaching office: infallible declarations by the Holy Father, like the recent dogma of the Assumption; ecumenical councils; creeds, like the Nicene Creed recited in the Mass; official catechisms; as well as the more intimate preaching of the clergy under the guidance of the bishops in every diocese.

But for the more valuable facets of Tradition the Church does turn to the past, namely, to the "Fathers of the Church." Commencing with the Apostolic Fathers, who had personal contact with the apostles or immediately followed them, the Church produced a series of illustrious leaders, renowned for learning and sanctity, who continued to hand down, through the early centuries, by their preaching and writings, the authentic truths revealed directly by Christ, or through His apostles, both those contained in the sacred books and those preached orally. Right here we see that there has always been a happy blending between Scripture and Tradition; some truths to be found in the written word, some in the spoken, many in both.

For the authentic interpretation of the mysteries of revelation we need sound guides. God has given us these holy and illustrious men, whom we call the Fathers and Doctors of the Church, those shining lights whom God willed to shine in the firmament of His Church, so that by means of them the darkness of the heretics might be dispelled. Men such as Irenaeus, Cyprian, Hilary, Athanasius, Basil, the two Gregorys, Ambrose, Jerome, Chrysostom, Augustine, Cyril. These and the Bishops and Shepherds, sober, learned, holy, who drank in the Catholic Faith with their mother's milk, drank it with their food, who have ministered this food and this drink to great and simple. It was by means of such planters, cultivators, and teachers, that, since the Apostles, the Church has grown.[3]

What gives tremendous weight to the authority of these Fathers is the harmonious agreement among them on the essential points of the revealed mysteries they have preserved.

God's greatest secret, that relating of His inner life, the sublime mystery of the Most Holy Trinity, we find especially detailed by the Fathers in Tradition, as well as in Scripture.

Theologians always draw first on these sources of our faith, on Scripture and Tradition, in formulating all the doctrines revealed by Christ to His one true Church. But to help us understand a little more clearly the doctrinal meaning of the mysteries of faith they often resort to analogies, comparisons, likenesses, similitudes to human ways of thinking and acting with which we are familiar. This should not surprise us. For did not the greatest Teacher make abundant use of such analogies? Recall His many parables: the mustard seed, the treasure hidden in a field, the pearl of great price, etc. The kingdom of heaven is like all these things, He said. In addition to such similitudes, Our Lord often cited examples from nature: "Consider the lilies of the field"; "You are the salt of the earth," etc. The story form of teaching was another favorite, classic examples of which are the parables of the Prodigal Son and the Good Samaritan. Why did Christ use this method so frequently? Because it well suited His purpose in conveying supernatural truths to His hearers in terms and figures that they easily understood.

It was only natural that the Fathers, in imitating the simplicity of the Gospel, found it helpful to resort to the appeal of analogies in explaining the Christian mysteries.

It is not surprising, then, that later theologians, including St. Thomas, had recourse to this method. For example, it helps us to see a similarity between the development of our supernatural growth in the Divine Life of grace and our natural growth from infancy to maturity. Thus baptism is rebirth, confirmation is soldiering, penance medicine, the Holy Eucharist nourishment. All these helps do not, however, detract from the tremendous mystery that is Divine Life, received and developed from the sacraments and added to our human nature, so that it participates in the very nature of God. But analogies do help, especially since we have to cooperate and make use of our supernatural powers, just as we make use of our natural powers and gifts of nature—body and mind.

So it is that when we come to the most sublime and important mystery of the Trinity—the secret of secrets—theologians make use of many human analogies in order to bring to our minds the fact that in one God there is a real Father, a real Son, and a real Person of Their mutual love. Their similitudes enable us to delve a bit more deeply into the secret of God's intimate life. From these analogies we could never discover the Trinity, but once we have learned about it from divine revelation they help us to acquaint ourselves more fully with it.

We must bear in mind that it was Christ Who revealed this secret to the apostles and that we find it recorded in the New Testament and authentically taught by the Fathers. It is only within the focus of the divine light of revelation that we find the story of the Divine Family and our incorporation into it. If we caught a bird's-eye view by a philosophical approach to the Divine Spirit in the preceding chapter, we merely add here and there the tiny tapers of human analogies in the following chapters, which serve to remove in some small way and only imperfectly the darkness of our feeble minds in the presence of this mystery—anticipating the destined day when we shall *see* the Father, Son, and Holy Spirit, face to face.

## *Notes*

1.      Dom Bernard Orchard, M.A., ed., *A Catholic Commentary on Holy Scripture* (New York: Nelson, 1951), p. 792.

2.      Tertullian, Adv. Prax., 31.

3.      St. Robert Bellarmine, *Sermons on the Doctors of the Church*, Roman Breviary, Feast.

# THREE

# Divine Persons

We can never hope to *understand* the mystery of the Trinity, but only to *explain* what God has revealed about it, to *us* and *for us*. If we do not think of the Father, Son, and Holy Spirit as Persons, the very names can become empty formulas. Beneath, behind the names, are personalities. Seeing that they *are* Persons helps us tremendously to understand what God intended us to understand in revealing the mystery. A personal God we could discover for ourselves; a Trinity of persons is the exciting secret God told us.

We would know that God must be a personal God. Surely we could never say that the divine nature knows and loves, but rather that God knows and loves— God, the Divine Spirit. Divine nature of itself, like human nature, is an abstract term. We never say John Smith's nature thought this or that; rather it was John Smith, the person, who thought. The same is true in speaking of God, *Who* knows and loves. Nature is *what* an individual has; person is *who* he is.

But within the divine nature there are *three* Divine Persons, not *one*. Christ referred to three personal names: Father, Son, Holy Spirit. Every priest, in the Athanasian creed which he recites in his office on Trinity Sunday, says: "And the Catholic Faith is this: that we worship God in Trinity, and Trinity in unity. Neither confusing the persons, nor dividing the nature. For there is one person of the Father, another of the Son, another of the Holy Spirit. But the Godhead of the Father and of the Son and of the Holy Spirit is but one, the glory equal and the majesty coeternal."

First of all, then, we should have a clear understanding of just what a person is. A simple definition would be that a person is the subject, possessor, proprietor, or "owner" of an individual rational nature that is distinct from every other possessor of a similar nature. For example, Michael the Archangel is the subject of an angelic nature. So is Gabriel. But Michael is definitely distinct from Gabriel, and this distinction, that he has in contrast to Gabriel and to all the other angels (each possessing an individual angelic nature), makes him a person. Or take the case of three individual men: John, James, Joseph. Each of these has an individual human nature (basically the same) but each possesses his own human nature in distinctly different ways from the others, according to his respective personality. Distinction in the way people "express" (possess) their human natures makes them persons. Therefore John's nature is slow-moving; James's animated and impetuous. John expresses himself with reserve; Joseph reveals himself as an open book. John is definitely not James or Joseph.

From this we see that a person is he who possesses an individual rational nature; his nature is *what* he possesses, body and soul. A person is the real self, always distinct from every other self. The admonition "Be yourself" is really quite useless. No one can possibly be other than himself, though he may imitate another. He must be content to be exclusively one person distinct from every other person in the world. From this it follows that no one can communicate or transfer his personality to anybody else. We can transfer the "ownership" of our house or car to another, but not that of our "personality" (or the ownership of our individual nature).

Being a person is really much more important than you probably think. If people realized the fact that this is a world made up of persons, it would certainly make for a better world than it is at the moment. For every person, from the very fact of being a person, necessarily carries with him a sublime dignity; that is to say, *every* person, be he king or pauper, poet or peasant, black or white. It is interesting to see how a person is "full of dignity," from the very root meaning and history of the word itself. Originally "person" signified a mask worn by Greek and Roman actors on the stage. These grotesque facial getups indicated whether an actor was impersonating a tragic or a comic character. There was a large opening at the mouth to let the voice resound through the audience. To "resound through" is from the Latin *personare*; hence the word *persona*, or person. Later this word signified the actor who portrayed some god, emperor, or character of distinction. Finally it referred to every human being as signifying dignity.

St. Thomas, the prince of theologians, says that "person signifies what is most perfect in all nature" and that "a person receives his distinction from all others primarily because of his 'high dignity.'"[1] Hence it is that

> a person is a noble, honorable, proprietor of all that he has and is. He is conscious of his essence and of the goods he possesses as well as of his proprietorship—full of enjoyment of proprietorship and possessions.... What is essential to personality is the dignity and worth of the person, owing to which he is deserving of respect in his possession and his being, as proprietor of a rational nature, even though he is not yet able to enjoy or exercise his proprietorship, or at any rate cannot fully enforce it externally. The former is the case of children who have not yet attained to the use of reason; the latter is the case with minors.[2]

We see a practical application of the "theology" involved in the meaning of person by contrast with the immorality of communism in the following quotation from Father Garrigou-Lagrange: "...person designates that which is superior in man, that by which man is ordered directly to God Himself above society. Thus, society, to which the individual is subordinate, is itself ordered to the full perfection of the human person, as against statism, which denies the higher rights of the human person."[3]

Now this explanation of the meaning of person as applied to angels and men gives us a lead in its reference to God. If every human person is of such outstanding distinction, how radiant and magnificent must a divine personality be! In addition to God having to be a person because He knows and loves, St. Thomas further says: "Person signifies...a free and intelligent subject [possessing] a rational nature."[4] He goes on to say that the term "person" most properly belongs to God, since the dignity of the divine nature exceeds every dignity, including the "high dignity" of a human person, referred to above.

The truth that Father, Son, and Holy Spirit are real Persons comes partly from what we saw about the way every spirit "acts"; partly from the meaning of person in general; but mostly from the very words of Christ, found in Sacred Scripture. God, then, being a spirit, knows and loves. Surely He knows Himself. But His knowledge of Himself differs decidedly from our knowledge of ourselves. The difference is this: our knowledge is not ourselves; we are not our thoughts. Our thoughts are what the philosophers call "accidental"; that is, they come and go and are merely so many operations of our mind. No thought of John Smith's would be identified as John Smith. But with God, Who is infinite simplicity, His thought *is* Himself, as also is each of His attributes.

Now we begin to discover the secret. God knows Himself, but this knowledge of Himself does not merely surpass, it totally transcends any knowledge of self possessed by angelic or human spirits. But, marvelous mystery, in expressing His thought of Himself He actually is the *Father* of this Thought. He expresses His thought of Himself inwardly, of course, in the mental Word. We find evidence for this, partly, in the sublime Gospel of St. John, the beloved disciple of Our Lord, who brought out the divinity of Christ more clearly than did the other Evangelists. You read this inspired passage of the New Testament at every Mass, at the Last Gospel: "In the beginning was the Word, and the Word was with God; and the Word was God" (John 1:1). We said that it is "partly" from St. John that we learn of God being the Father of His thought of Himself. St. John's inspired evidence tells us that God "expressed" His thought in a "Word" Who was God, distinct from the Father. It is from Christ we learn how truly God is the Father of His thought. For Christ, the Son of God, said: "From God I came forth" (John 8:24).

From these inspired texts it is clear that in God we have a Father expressing Himself, forming a concept of Himself, which concept is His Son.

But something even more wonderful takes place within this inner life of God. Besides knowing, God also loves, as we saw. Naturally a divine Father and Son must love each other. In Their mutual love we learn the remainder of the secret. For this expression of Their mutual love is another Person, called the Holy Spirit. Again, Christ tells us this. "And I will ask the Father and he will give you another Advocate" (John 14:16), and "when the Advocate has come, whom I will send you from the Father, the Spirit of truth, who proceeds from the Father, he will bear witness concerning me" (John 15:26).

Now these processions of the Son and the Holy Spirit mentioned by Christ result in Their being real Persons. St. Thomas draws from the philosophical definition of persons as applied to angels and men, and applies this explanation to Divine Persons.[5] To put it as simply as possible, because the Son proceeds from the Father, and the Holy Spirit proceeds from both the Father and the Son, there necessarily follow definite "relations" between Them. That is to say, there is the relation of fatherhood between the Father and Son; a relation of sonship between the Son and the Father; a relation of mutual love between the Father-Son and Their common Spirit of Love.

In these most intimate of relations, the Father communicates to the Son His entire divine nature as He expresses Him in a mental Word; and the Father and Son communicate Their entire divine nature to Their mutual expression of Love for one another. This communication of the divine nature must take place, because of the simplicity of this nature which can in no way be divided among the Three (Thinker, Thought, and Love). In this communication the Father pours everything, all He has in the Godhead, into the manifestation of His Thought, holding nothing back. The same is true with Father and Son. They pour the totality of Their Divine Love into one another. What They cannot communicate are the relations of fatherhood, sonship, and lovingness.[6] These are distinct and proper respectively to Father, Son, and Holy Spirit. And since we have only this triple distinction in God, whereby each Person is a co-possessor of one and the same nature, in three different ways, we have what our former definition requires for persons.

These personal relationships exist in the utter simplicity of God. Unlike the attributes or perfections, which are not distinct, but divinely blended, the Persons are definitely individual. "This question of the relations, as explained by St. Thomas, is of the greatest importance...it throws light on the entire treatise of the Trinity."[7]

These processions within the Godhead reveal what theologians call the "fecundity" of the divine nature. For us, it means that there are three magnificent personalities—three real, intensely lovable Persons in God. Because Father, Son, and Holy Spirit possess the one identical nature, this makes for the greatest intimacy between Them. Theologians refer to this intimacy as the divine society, fellowship, communion, and companionship. But what term is more apt than the "Divine Family," used frequently by Philipon and d'Eypernon?[8]

Surely everybody has "relatives." But what relations are more intimate than those between the members of a family? What closer relations[9] can you have than a Father, a Son, and a third member that is divinely unique, Their mutual Love, so personal that it *is* a Person? Here we have a Family "united" in *one* nature, *one* mind, *one* capacity for love; but a Family of divinely individual personalities, with the "expressive" personality of a Speaker, the "expressed" personality of a Word, and the "manifesting" personality of Love; a Family divinely united in divinely distinct personalities; a Family where the Father eternally utters His Word, where Father and Son eternally love, where the Person of Love eternally binds Father to Son!

## *Notes*

1.  *Summa*, I, Q. 29, Art. 3.
2.  Matthias J. Scheeben, *The Mysteries of Christianity* (St. Louis: Herder, 1946), p. 72.
3.  Reginald Garrigou-Lagrange, O.P., *The Trinity and God the Creator* (St. Louis: Herder, 1952), p. 156.
4.  *Summa*, I, Q. 29, Art. 3.
5.  *Summa*, I, Qs. 27, 28, 29.
6.  Apt term used by Frank Sheed in his excellent treatment of the Trinity in *Theology and Sanity* (Sheed & Ward, 1946), p. 82.
7.  Garrigou-Lagrange, *op. cit.*, p. 109.
8.  M. M. Philipon, O.P., *The Sacraments in the Christian Life* (Westminster, Md.: Newman Press, 1955); Taymans d'Eypernon, S.J., *The Blessed Trinity and the Sacraments* (Westminster, Md.: Newman Press, 1961).
9.  Theologically, "relations" in the Trinity are the existing relationships between Father, Son, and Holy Spirit, which relationships, though distinct from each other, yet identified with the divine nature, constitute the Persons in God. By a play of words we use "relations" in this context, also, as by extension, in comparison with members of a family who are both relations (relatives) and persons at the same time. The extension is valid because the Divine Persons *are related*. However, it must be clearly understood that the Holy Spirit is a Person unique in the fellowship of the Trinity, having no counterpart in a human family.

# FOUR

# *Father*

To address a person by name makes him aware of his importance as an individual. It accentuates the dignity belonging to him, and to no one else in the world. There may be a hundred John Smiths in the telephone directory, but when you address one of them by name, you identify him as a person; his dignity belongs to him alone and not to any other John Smith. A similar name may belong to others, but the dignity is distinct.

So, too, when we make a "person-to-person" phone call, the name is important. How ever would we reach the person except by name?

A name, then, indicates the person and distinguishes him from all others. Thus when someone gives his personal name, he stands out from the crowd. Without a name the person loses his identity. His name forces you to recognize his person. A clear example of this appears in the case of records. A name is essential to identify a person for issuing (and referring to) a birth certificate, baptismal record, naturalization papers, and driver's license.

Now the name, father, is significant in identifying a particular father of a particular son. And the Divine Father has this same significance in relation to the Son, because He is His Father in the most perfect sense of the term. But besides being a generic term (father-son relationship), Father in the Trinity is a most *personal* name, distinguishing a Divine Person, with all His exalted dignity, from the other two Persons. This distinction, as we saw, consists solely in the divine paternity. The personal name of Father is most appropriate then, because the Father really begets or "generates" the Son.

It would be well to remember that there is more than one way of "giving birth," even on the human level. In the first place, both in the human world as well as in the animal kingdom, generation of offspring signifies the "production" of one living being from another in such a way that the offspring is always similar to the parents.

But on the human level we have another kind of so-called generation, not physical but mental, where we see, on a higher plane, fruitful production resulting in similarity of nature between the producer and the product. When we say a man "conceives" an idea, we mean that he gives birth to an idea. The very word "concept," or idea, brings this out. Concept comes from the Latin word *concipere*, which means to conceive. While conception is only the first stage in physical generation, the term "concept" indicates, by extension, that when a man produces an idea he generates (in a broad sense) a thought. In fact, one meaning of "conceive" is "to take into one's mind; to form a mental image; to think." What is more, there is a striking similarity between the thought and the mind. Both are spiritual. Remember, man's soul is a spirit. His power of knowing, as well as the resulting thought, must be spiritually similar.

This idea of analogous generation is all the clearer, and very apt for what follows, when we consider a man forming a thought about himself. Here the man forms a mental image of himself in which he really recognizes himself. His mind becomes a mirror wherein he sees himself. But the image is not a static image such as the looking glass gives. On the contrary, it is a living image, because it is a spiritual act. But, of course, this living image does not have a separate life apart from the nature of the man, as does a child who is similar to its parents and yet has a separate human nature all its own. The man's thought of himself is purely "accidental." It comes and goes. When present, it always remains within his mind, not apart from it.

But in God we have a far more perfect kind of generation than in the physical production of offspring or the mental production by the human mind. For as the Son "proceeds," the Father (as we saw) communicates not a "similar" nature but His identical divine nature to the Son, Who, as the "uttered" Word, possesses divine life equally with the Father. This fact of divine generation adds further meaning to the secret, that God does not live a lonely life.

In seeing how His name so well fits the Divine Father (because He generates a Son), we can do no better than turn to St. Thomas.[1] He shows beautifully from texts of Sacred Scripture how we have an example of perfect intellectual generation, when the Father in knowing Himself expresses this knowledge in the Word, His Son, and indicates how, when He produces Him, He really generates a Son. Here St. Thomas lets the Son tell us of His generation from the Father, first, in echoes from certain passages of the Old Testament (containing the first faint hints of the secret), which detail for us the parallel stages of physical generation, but show how generation in God needs no stages.

The following is a summary of St. Thomas. The first quotation shows that the Father conceives a Son: "The depths were not as yet, and I was already conceived" (Proverbs 8:24). The manner in which the Father really "conceives" a Son is, of course, divinely different from human conception. In the latter case, once the embryo beings to exist, it must remain within the womb some time before actual birth. In God, there is no time element, as the phrase "the depths were not as yet" (from eternity) indicates. However, the Son is (but remains) eternally within the Father, for as St. John assures us, He "is in the bosom of the Father" (John 1:18). We see that there is no distinction between conception and birth when the Father begets His Son, from the verse quoted above from the Book of Proverbs and from the verse that follows: " Before the hills, I was brought forth" (Proverbs 8:25). Here again we have another poetic reference to eternity, in "before the hills." Psalm 109, verse 3, shows again that conception and birth are the same when the Father says (in another hint): "From the womb before the [eternal] day star I begot thee."

In the case of human parents this wonder —savoring of the miraculous—of conceiving and finally giving birth, as fruit in the mystery of human love, reaches its pinnacle when the infant child lies present before its parents. So, in closing his parallel between divine and human generation, St. Thomas quotes verse 27 of chapter 8 of Proverbs: "When he prepared the heavens, I was present." The main impact of the text, of course, according to St. Thomas, is to "preclude any notion that the Son did not exist while He was being brought forth."

The Psalms again furnish perhaps the most intimate and "fatherly" of texts: "Thou art my son, this day have I begotten thee" (Psalms 2:7). Then turning to the more familiar passages of the New Testament, we find what always sounds like a haunting refrain, as we hear it at the close of every Mass: "and we saw his glory— glory as of the only-begotten of the Father" (John 1:14). Again in St. John we read the quotation from the favorite disciple that tenderly describes the intimacy of love between the Father and the Son—diffusive intimacy that carries over to us: "For God so loved the world, that he gave his only-begotten Son" (John 3:16).

And there you have it: God Himself tells us that as a real Father He generates His Son.

But this secret, unlike human ones, preserves its wonder forever. We do not have to recapture, in memory, the magic spell its first telling cast over us. And why is this? Because, as already indicated, the Father is ever generating His Son. With God there is no past nor future. It is not that this divine birth took place "before the hills" were made. It occurs "in the one unique instant of eternity"—the stable now, not fluent as time. The intellect and the will of God are always in action. Therefore the divine intellect is never without the Word, nor is the divine will ever without personal love, or the Holy Spirit.

The eternity of the divine generation makes it easy to understand what St. Thomas tells us, then, about the Father being the "origin" or "principle" of the Trinity. Since there is no question of any priority of time in God, we understand by "origin" that the Father is the source from Whom the Son and the Holy Spirit proceed. They proceed as simultaneously from Their source as heat and light do from the sun. It is in this sense then that we refer to the Father as the First Person of the Blessed Trinity; first, only because His Word and Love proceed from Him, not because He existed first.

Delightful, as a sort of added surprise contained in the secret, is the corollary or conclusion that Father Garrigou-Lagrange points out in his explanation of St. Thomas's treatise on the Trinity: "A great joy rises from this eternal generation. Vestiges of this joy are found in the mother when a child is born to her."[2] The surprise is that we see *joy* in God. Do we ever think of this? Joy seems too human for God. Yet every human joy is but a faint glimmer of divinely intense joy necessarily contained in the very essence of God's nature. Could not the Son of God, then, have recalled His Father's joy when He tenderly portrayed a mother thus: "when she has brought forth the child, she no longer remembers the anguish for her joy that a man is born into the world" (John 16:21)?

The Divine Father should ever remain intimate and familiar to us (and impart to us His joy) because of the immortal tribute to His fatherliness given by St. Paul: "I bend my knees to the Father of Our Lord Jesus Christ, from whom all fatherhood in heaven and on earth receives its name" (Ephesians 3:14–15). Father Garrigou-Lagrange expands this thought with warmth that extols, as extending from the Divine, every human kind of "father" that we know.

> From the height of this mystery light falls on the words of St. Paul.... For from the divine paternity is derived that spiritual paternity by which the Supreme Pontiff is Father of the Christian people, by which the founder of a religious order is the father of his sons, by which the Bishop is father is his diocese, and by which the priest is the father of souls committed to his care. From this divine paternity, too, is derived that earthly paternity, which is something noble and excellent in the good Christian father, who like a patriarch gives his sons and daughters not only corporal life but heavenly blessings as did Abraham, Isaac and Jacob.[3]

Holding on to this lower note in the scale of paternity, we can amplify it a moment and then soar back to the heights of divine fatherhood.

There is one thing that stands out as belonging uniquely to the ideal father of a family: he is the provider. As the mother is the heart that molds the children, the father is the head that plans ways and means to support and provide for every need. He is (or should be) the chief breadwinner. He is the planner who looks ahead at long range in considering what is expendable at the moment. He foresees family needs of the future, ensuring for emergencies and saving for necessary expansions as the family grows and develops. The ideal Christian family recognizes this role of the father and counts on him for the security that they sense he stands for.

That this is a Godlike role in the human father follows naturally from St. Paul's tribute, when on bended knees he recognized that human fatherhood is "named" after the fatherhood of God. In looking from the created father to the uncreated prototype we must see this creaturely reflection of "providingness" intensified to divine dimensions in God the Father. We call this Divine Providence. It is an attribute of the Deity that we like to think of as especially referring to the Father.

Providence means seeing ahead. That is why providing looks to the future and requires broad vision. We can easily imagine, from the need of providing for a family, what tremendous vision would be needed to provide for a world. Because God wisely governs the world He created, according to His divine sense of order, St. Thomas says that He does so with Divine Providence, quoting from the Book of Wisdom: "But thy providence, O Father, governeth it" (Wisdom 14:3).[4]

If there is one attribute of the Father we seem to take for granted, it is His providence. How bewildering it would be to try to count the infinite variety, to say nothing of the inexhaustible supply, of goods He continually lavishes on the world for the use and enjoyment of the children of men! Since God made us with bodies, He knew we would get thirsty and hungry, would need clothes and tools. So, as a provident Father, He provides the necessities of life which the author of Ecclesiasticus lists for us: "The principal things necessary for the life of men, are water, fire, and iron, salt, milk, and bread of flour, and honey, and the cluster of the grape, and oil, and clothing" (Ecclesiasticus 39:31).

The Father knew we needed food for the mind, as well. And He provided "knowledge of the things that are: to know the disposition of the whole world, and the virtues of the elements, the beginning, and ending, and midst of the times, the alterations of their courses, and the changes of the seasons, the revolutions of the year, and the disposition of the stars" (Wisdom 7:17–19). (In the excitement of discovering outer space, we do well to consider Who created it—and why.)

To brighten our way and relieve the monotony of daily existence, Divine Providence added the tonic of beauty: for men who till the land to see "the beauty of the field" (Psalms 49:11); during resting time to wonder at "the circle of the stars, or the great water, or the sun and moon" (Wisdom 13:2); and for inspiration, to join David and lift up our "eyes to the mountains" (Psalms 120:1).

Providence has also apportioned "A time to weep, and a time to laugh: a time to mourn, and a time to dance" (Ecclesiastes 3:4). This is why the Father further implanted the playful instinct in the children of men, who from infancy naturally play and laugh and sing. And all these provisions—for free—we take so casually, the while we complain!

The big complaint is that the Father assigned "a time to weep." In other words, how do we reconcile Fatherly blessings with suffering? The answer is: there are blessings "dressed for the part" and there are "blessings in disguise." Both come from the Father. In the first place, when God created the world it was a garden where there was nothing to cause tears. Foolish man "imported" a lot of things that caused weeping. Now that these are always with us, the Father can convert them into good —good for us—just as He did for David: "Thou hast turned for me my mourning into joy" (Psalms 29:12).

David is a witness, if you are looking for a "case history." If you want a theologian, St. Augustine tells us that "since God is the highest good, He would in no way allow anything evil in His works, unless He were so omnipotent and so good that He could make good come from evil."[5] (For example, "there would not be the patience of the martyrs unless there were the iniquity of the persecutor.") If you want a bit of homespun theology: Our lives are like tapestries; we see the rough side, all covered with knots; God sees (in process) the finished side (which we shall see by reflection when we see the whole secret in vision).

But it is the Son of God Who best points out the loving providence of the Father that covers our entire lives. For an example, by the way, He calls attention to some of the "extras" provided for our sheer delight. In the sublime Sermon on the Mount (in Matthew, Chapter 6) He refers to the Father ten times, including the perfect prayer where He teaches us to ask the Father for our daily bread. Then, with due emphasis on "first things first," he tell us that instead of getting worried over material needs, we should trust in the Father's providence:

> Therefore I say to you, do not be anxious for your life, what you shall eat; nor yet for your body, when you shall put on.... Look at the birds of the air: they do not sow, or reap, or gather into barns; yet your heavenly Father feeds them.... And as for clothing, why are you anxious? See how the lilies of the field grow; they neither toil nor spin, yet I say to you that not even Solomon in all his glory was arrayed like one of these.... Therefore do not be anxious, saying, 'What shall we eat?' or, 'What shall we drink?' or, 'What shall we put on?'" (for after all these things the Gentiles seek); for your Father knows that you need all these things. But seek first the kingdom of God and his justice, and all these things shall be given you besides (Matthew 6:25, 26, 28–29, 31–33).

It is therefore fitting, as St. Paul exhorts us, that we "walk worthily of God, and please him in all things…joyfully rendering thanks to the Father" (Colossians 1:10, 12).

## *Notes*

1. *Contra Gentes*, IV, C. II.
2. Reginald Garrigou-Lagrange, O.P., *The Trinity and God the Creator* (St. Louis: Herder, 1952), p. 94.
3. *Op. cit.*, pp. 206–207.
4. *Summa*, II, Q. 103, Art. 1.
5. *Enchiridion*, Chap. II.

## *Son*

To identify the Second Person of the Holy Trinity we have three names: Word, Image, Son. We have already seen that the Father generates His Son as His Word. In case this name seems too impersonal or unappealing, we have only to recall the opening of St. John's Gospel. Here St. John the Divine—"who is reluctant to dwell upon the earth, riding like an eagle to the highest heavens, to tell us what takes place in the sanctuary of the divinity"[1] —uses the term "Word" exclusively. The reading of this chapter sounds like something in a divine rather than in a human vernacular. Set in such an idiom, this name emerges as most personal: "In the beginning was the Word, and the Word was with God; and the Word was God.... And the Word was made flesh and dwelt among us" (John 1:1, 14).

Intimacy also appears in this name, because of the close relation between the divine mind and the procession therefrom of the Father's uttered thought of Himself. And because, as we saw, this procession is a real intellectual generation, the Father's Word *is* His Son. And how can the Word appear *impersonal* when He is a *Person*!

Moreover, the Word is not in any sense a silent or inactive Person. His Personality is as vital as the Father's, having all the divine vitality of the same divine nature that the Father communicates to Him, making Him a co-possessor, with all the dignity of a distinct Person. Far from being silent, the Word is most "expressive." He is a Person precisely because in Him the Father utters, enunciates, *expresses* His very self. Nor must we think of the Word as merely being passively expressed. Rather, He eternally expresses the Father—manifests and reflects Him within the sanctuary of the Divine Family. All this marvelous "fecundity" takes place, we must remember, in the inner life of God.

But another surprise! We also come into the divine picture. And we do so in the focus of the Word. For, as St. Thomas reminds us, "the Word implies relation to creatures, as well as to the Father,"[2] and he explains for us that God, besides knowing Himself, necessarily knows every creature He created. We, of course, have to use almost a full dictionary of words to express all kinds of different things. With God, it is entirely different, because He, by one act, understands Himself and all things. And since the Word contains the entire content of the divine knowledge, which the Father communicates to Him, this one single Word expresses the knowledge of us as well as of the Father and all things known by Them. So we see that the term "Word" designates the special function of manifesting: first, the Father's knowledge of Himself; second, all things (ourselves included) known in the vast depths of the divine mind. The Word is, then, the personal, divine utterance of the Father. As Ecclesiasticus puts it, "I came out of the mouth of the Most High" (Ecclesiasticus 24:5).

Divine Image, as a name, appears even more intimate and reminds us of the use of this term as applied to a human son. How many times we hear the expression, "He is the perfect image of his father!" And we can say this of every son in a very real sense. For no matter whether a particular boy may have a crop of flaming red hair, while his father (if he has any) has coal-black hair, yet this son has to be an image of his father. This results from the very fact of human generation, by which something of the nature of the father passes over to the son, and the son bears a resemblance or likeness to the father because he inherits the same kind of human nature; but this likeness comes mainly as a result of descending (proceeding) from the father who is his origin. In fact, every son is a sort of resemblance of his father. And parents, in generating offspring, expect to produce children who will be "like" them.

Now we see this same pattern of generation in the Divine Father and Son. The Father, in begetting His Word, generates His Image—a real, living, personal Image of Himself. Actually Word, Image, and Son are one and the same in God. But the wealth of meaning implied in divine Sonship cannot be brought out in one term. So we have three terms to designate the fruitfulness of God's paternity.

As we said before, when a man thinks about himself he not only has a thought of himself but also an image in the mirror of his mind. The same thing happens in the divine mind. The Father expresses the Thought of Himself in His Word which, because of its divine likeness to Himself, is His Image. He "expresses" His Word and "impresses" His Image.

The Father not only knows Himself in His Word, but He sees Himself mentally in His Image. He recognizes here all His divine perfections mirrored in the Person Who is the Image He begot by transmitting, not part of, but His entire, identical nature to another Person, Who is like the Father in all respects save that of the divine paternity. He recognizes His divine counterpart. The Word is His "spokesman"; the Image is His "mirror."

Scripture is aglow with references to the Divine Image: "unspotted mirror of God's majesty, and the image of his goodness" (Wisdom 7:26); "the brightness of his glory and the image of his substance" (Hebrews 1:3); "image of the invisible God" (Colossians 1:15).

But Son is the favorite name. We might call this the first name, the Word and Image secondary ones —explanatory names, if you will. Son is certainly the most proper and personal name. It signifies the familiarity and endearment known in human sonship, but here intensified to the divine degree and really incapable of measure or comparison. A feeble attempt would be to say that the difference between night and day completely misses the mark as a comparison of the joy attending the news that a certain man is a father for the first time, and the "announcement" that God the Father has a Son. And this is an eternal announcement, engraved (for us) in the inspired phrase: "Though art my son, this day I have begotten thee" (Psalms 2:7).

Too often we think of God's Son in terms of His incarnate life. Too often we see the human in place of the divine nature. To do this is to miss the whole purpose of the Incarnation. It is of the utmost importance that we remember that the life of the Son is eternal. His cure of the blind man, healing of a woman's hemorrhage, restoration to health of ten lepers, bringing Lazarus back to life, and the feeding of five thousand people with five fish and two loaves of bread, are all evidence of His divinity. "Human" compassion was a means to let some rays of divine light shine through. Magdalene saw this light in His eyes. Peter, James, and John saw it in His face and garments on the heights of Tabor, and fainted dead away. One of the soldiers recognized it after the crime of deicide on Calvary, when he exclaimed, "Truly this man was the Son of God" (Mark 15:39).

As Father Meschler says: "The life of the Divine Person and Nature of our Lord and Saviour and this life of His before the creation is far more sublime and significant than His temporal life.... As far as God is above creatures, so far is this divine life of the God-Man above His created life."[3]

When Christ was only twelve years old He made the first public announcement of His main purpose for coming on earth: "Did you not know that I must be about my Father's business?" (Luke 2:49). His "Father's business" was to manifest the Father and lead us to Him; to lead us to the Father by the security of grace here, which ensures leading us in glory hereafter. The more we know of our destination the more eagerly we shall anticipate "arriving" and strive to earn a richer participation in its joys by gaining bigger dividends of the happiness for which we were made.

How thoroughly Christ accomplished His business we see from over two hundred references to the Father recorded in the New Testament. The Son stressed over and over again that He came from the Father and that He was returning to Him—but not "empty-handed." In the touching scene of His farewell supper with His intimate friends He let His human feelings express the very intimate experience of nostalgia: "Father, the hour has come! Glorify thy Son, that thy Son may glorify thee.... And now do thou, Father, glorify me with thyself, with the glory that I had with thee before the world existed" (John 17:1, 5).

Not only are there numerous texts definitely referring to the Father but the entire content of the New Testament unfolds the doctrine of the Blessed Trinity. Would you not say, then, that it is highly purposeful to know as much as possible of this life of the Son within the Divine Family from whence He came, to which He returned, and where He awaits our arrival?

Again we turn to St. John for the perfect text. In the concluding verse of his first chapter, on the Word, he says: "No one has at any time seen God. The only-begotten Son, who is in the bosom of the Father, he has revealed Him" (John 1:18). What more intimate an expression than "in the bosom of the Father"! This is no mere fanciful figure of speech. On the contrary, it clearly brings out the intimacy that really exists between the Son and His Father within the divine nature—intimacy possible only in the Divine Family.

We say that we tenderly hold or clasp someone to our bosom, but this is woefully inadequate for a Father and Son Who are divine. God the Father has no need to "hold" His Son, Who is *within* the Godhead equally with Himself, because the Father communicated to His Son not a similar but His identical nature. "Bosom" in a human father signifies the region of the heart, the seat of love. God has no need for a heart. "Bosom" in God signifies His inner nature. In this nature God's love *is* God. Tenderness in human love is but the weakest reflection of the overwhelming love that is divine—divinely indescribable.

"In the bosom" not only describes the divine intimacy between the Son and His Father, but the very word "intimacy" finds its most perfect example here. This word comes from the Latin *intimus*, that is, pertaining to the innermost nature of a thing. There is no greater degree of "innermost" than a Son Who is identical with the nature of His Father—Who is in the Father.

We saw from those poignant words uttered at the Last Supper, referring to the "glory that I had with thee before the world existed," that the Son of God did not commence His life on a winter night in Bethlehem. Rather, He is in the bosom of the Father eternally. And, as a matter of fact, He never departed from this divine embrace. Part of the stupendous mystery is that, from the moment He opened His eyes in the manger till He closed them in agony on the Cross, He was in the bosom of the Father. The staggering fact is that time did not interrupt eternity but blended with it.

It is wonderful indeed to see the Son in the flesh when we open to the greatest story ever told, but the ravishing news contained in the secret about divine life in the bosom of the Father is all the more full of wonder for us. To spell out this wonder was the reason for the Son's coming in the flesh—to spell it out so clearly that we would remember it and look forward to seeing it with clearer vision than is possible to mortal eyes.

Now we know the Son not as thirty-three years of age, nor as He is in the centuries-old life of the Mystical Body, but we see Him within the Divine Family as ageless as the eternity that He *is*. Above the realm of time, the eternal joy of "Thou art my son" (Psalms 2:7) blends with the divine echo, "Thou art my father" (Psalms 88:27). We, too, enter into this divine joy. Else why did They communicate such knowledge to us? We, too, can shake off the shackles of time! In fact, we can see ourselves with the Son "in the bosom of the Father." All this may seem dreamlike, but it is very real. For the Son as the Word of God knew us; we were included with His knowledge of all creatures in the divine mind. And the only "place" we could be present was "in the bosom of the Father." We saw ourselves as known to God, in the first chapter when we read of God as a Spirit Who "knows" and Whose inner life is even more intriguing than His external activity. We saw ourselves as "thoughts," in the Word. But seeing ourselves in the divine bosom we begin to discover that we must be "brothers" of the Son—we must have been brothers for a long, long time, even before time began! We see ourselves as planned for divine brotherhood, with all the dignity of persons with individual names—each soul important and nobody insignificant. Eternally planned, with eternal destiny in the eternal bosom!

## *Notes*

1. Dom Columba Marmion, *Christ and His Mysteries* (St. Louis: Herder, 1939), p. 36.
2. *Summa*, II, Q. 34, Art. 3.
3. Maurice Meschler, s.j., The Life of Our Lord (St. Louis: Herder, 1928), p. 25.

## SIX

# *Breathing Bond of Love*

Penetrating further through the veil that conceals the secret, we discover within the Spirit, Who is God, that the Father and the Son, besides knowing each other with divine familiarity, must love, with the same divine intensity, the Infinite Goodness They mutually behold: "The Father loves the Son" (John 3:35); "I love the Father" (John 14:31).

It is because the Father and Son "know" each other with such divine intimacy and recognize in this mutual knowledge all Their divine goodness, that Their consequent joy bursts into a transport of Love (every spirit knows and loves). And as we are led further *within* the intimate life of the Divine Family, we are introduced to the Third Person of the Holy Trinity Whose personality is *expressive* of this interior movement of love that flows eternally within the Godhead.

And what is the identifying name of this most expressive personality within the family circle? St. Thomas tells us that He really has no proper name. So we have rather to "invent" one—not one, but several "accommodated" or appropriate names. This very indefiniteness delightfully preserves the sense of mystery in the secret.

Regarding the name, Holy Spirit, St. Thomas says: "While there are two processions in God, one of these, the procession of love, has no proper name of its own. Hence the relations also which follow from this procession are without a name: for this reason the Person proceeding in that manner has no proper name. But as some names are accommodated by the usual manner of speaking to signify the aforesaid relations, as when we use the names of procession and spiration...to signify the divine Person Who proceeds by way of love, this name Holy Spirit is by the use of scriptural speech accommodated to Him. The appropriateness of this name may be shown...from the fact that the Person Who is called Holy Spirit has something in common with the other Persons. For, as St. Augustine says, 'Because the Holy Spirit is common to both, He Himself is called that properly which both are called in common. For the Father also is a spirit, and the Son is a spirit; and the Father is holy, and the Son is holy.'" [1]

And right here we see that if Holy Spirit lacks the characteristic of being a proper name in the same sense that Father and Son are, it nevertheless is most meaningful as a descriptive name. What it lacks in "properness," it makes up in significance, in describing the manner in which the Father and Son "express" Their mutual love. So it is that, as we call the procession of the Second Person "generation," we refer to that of the Third Person as "spiration" or a breathing-forth. And while Love, as we shall soon see, is another name referring to the Third Person, we must always understand that it is Love breathed-forth. For it is precisely because He results from this act of *spiration* that the Holy Spirit is a Person distinct from the Father and the Son.

In *Mysteries of Christianity* Father Scheeben writes:

> The sigh which proceeds from the mutual love of the First Person and His personal Word is necessarily something other than these two Persons, Who pour forth Their love and the real content of Their love into Him with the goodness of Their essence.... The sigh of the divine love is therefore a personal sigh, a Person, and a Person distinct from Them Who breathe Him forth in Their love. This sigh is not only a manifestation of the love of two hearts for each other (as in human love) which wish their life, their ardor, to flow over to each other. It is a sigh in which two divine Persons, out of the absolute oneness and full-ness of Their common 'heart' prove Their love with utter efficacy, in that They transmit this oneness to a third Person.[2]

In calling the Holy Spirit the "Divine Sigh," Father Scheeben (with others) compares this breathing-forth of love to a gentle exhalation of the breath, by which human lovers often manifest their love. We observe this plaintive sigh of the lover especially when the lover is separated from the beloved, or when the beloved receives a gift from the lover.

In borrowing from human manifestations of love, the Fathers and Doctors go further than the sigh, even to the *kiss* of love. Thus St. Augustine, bringing out the thought previously expressed by his teacher, St. Ambrose, calls the product of the second procession in God "communion, embrace, kiss, bond, unity; by which the two are joined together and preserve Their unity of Spirit in the bond of peace."[3] Likewise, St. Bernard calls the Holy Spirit "the most sweet kiss of the Father and Son, because He is both the mutual knowledge and love of the Father and Son. Their bond of union, Their singular love."[4] It is, of course, the kiss that seals the sigh of human love.

While the human sigh of love is a gentle thing, there is nothing gentle about the outpouring of divine love. This is rather something torrential—Niagara-like. Father Scheeben has a magnificent passage explaining this:

> The word *procedere* (to proceed) means primarily a movement from one place to another; ...the analogy of movement applies to the spiration of the Holy Spirit in a special way. He is movement in His very being, as it were, just as love is. In the procession of the Holy Spirit the Father and Son commune with each other; there is an eternal surrendering and accepting in the most liberal sense, an infi-

nitely powerful living breath which emanates from one to the other and from both the mighty pulsation of an infinite heart which surges with the supreme ardor of affection, the blazing flame of an infinite fire of love. There is, in brief, the intensity, the activity, the effusion and the torrent of love in which the Father and Son fuse and pour forth Their nature into the Holy Spirit. This is why the Holy Spirit is symbolized by the roaring of the wind which shook the house of the apostles on Pentecost, and in the darting flaming tongues that hovered over their heads. This is why the Savior compares Him to a brimming stream of living water: "He who believes in me...from within him there shall flow rivers of living water"; whereupon St. John adds: "Now this he said of the Spirit which they should receive" (John 7:38–39). Therefore when we say that the Holy Spirit proceeds from the Father and the Son, we mean not only that He has His origin from Them, but that this origin takes place in the manner of an out-gushing movement, which is accomplished in the effusion of love and the donation of life from the Father and the Son to the Holy Spirit.[5]

What Father Scheeben develops with such imaginative warmth, the Liturgy says with exquisite poetic economy in the "Veni Creator":

> Thou who art called the Paraclete,
> Best gift of God above,

> The living spring, the living fire,
> Sweet unction, and true love!

Thus we see from all this figurative description, the wealth of meaning contained in the appropriated names of the Third Person Who is breathed forth like wind, flame, and flood, which, indefinite though they may be, are in the words of Father Scheeben, "all the richer in coloring and vividness."[6]

St. Bernard reminds us, however, that though this divine outpouring seems to imply something torrential in human terms, it is far from being violent or feverish. Rather it savors of the utmost calm wherein is found "imperturbable peace."[7]

The second appropriate name for the Third Person is Love—but "love proceeding." Love, as a personal name, is not as concrete as Word, for the Son. But this is as it should be, because the act of loving necessarily lacks the definiteness of a thought produced in the mind. Love which proceeds from the will is too vague to express in a definite word. This is why we say that love is "ineffable," or unutterable, indefinable. This is the reason why lovers resort to the figurative language of poetry to express the affections of their hearts. The Holy Spirit is Love that "proceeds" from the Father and the Son. Love is in the *Person* of the sigh, the flame, etc. It is of the utmost importance, then, that when we refer to the Third Person as the "Love" of the Father and the Son we do not imply the "essential" love which is a perfection in the divine nature, which Love *is* God. But we refer to the

Love "breathed-forth" Who is a Person in the Divine Family—with one of His personal names being Love.

Because of the intimate relation of the Holy Spirit to the Father and the Son, He is called the *Bond* between Them. In human parlance a bond is a tie which unites. We often speak of the bond of love that unites lovers, which a ring so well symbolizes. But between the two Divine Persons there is a Bond Who is a living, breathing, real Person! Into this Person They pour the entire content of Their mutual love and bliss—all the divine wealth of the nature They have in common. Instead of having to resort to the feebleness of an embrace, as with human lovers, They eternally gaze at another Person and see Themselves united in the manner that is uniquely divine—in the bond which closes the family circle.

Another personal name for the Holy Spirit is Gift. All lovers give gifts to each other. This constitutes a "language" that lovers understand. It may be diamonds; it may be trinkets. The value of the gift consists in the love content. The giving of gifts, universal among lovers, has its origin in God. "The reason of a gift is love.... Hence it is manifest that love has the nature of a first gift, through which all free gifts are given."[8] The Holy Spirit is the Gift of Father to Son, and of Son to Father.

A gift implies an aptitude to be given, and what is given has a certain relation both to the giver and to the one to whom a gift is given. No one could give a gift unless it was his to give; and a gift is given to someone to be his, for his enjoyment. So the Holy Spirit "belongs" to both the Father and the Son, because by His divine origin He is "related" to both. Furthermore, there is always a certain identity between the giver and the gift. As it is true that the gift we give to another is more valuable according to how much of ourselves we put into the gift, it is divinely more valuable when the Father and the Son put Their "all" into the love They mutually pour forth in the "Gift" Who is the Holy Spirit. It is in and through this Person-Gift that They eternally love one another.

And now the ecstatic (throwing us out of ourselves) point of the secret! We could somehow grasp the fact that we are eternally in the divine mind of the Father, and in the divine bosom with the Son, but that They would not keep this divine Gift exclusively for Themselves seems beyond comprehension. St. Thomas tells us that the Father and the Son give this most divinely personal Gift to *us*! Again, "Love does such things." We are said to possess what we can freely use and enjoy as we please, and the Father and the Son love us with the same Divine Person that They each love. But since we could never attain the possession and consequent enjoyment thereof by our own efforts, this lavish donation must be a real "Gift," Who gives Himself with the other two.

We really do not need a theologian as witness for this fact. Nor do we need an artist. For what human artistic genius could ever capture the divine content in the wistful expression of the Son, as He sat by the well, parched with thirst (not so much human as divine), and exclaimed to the Samaritan woman: "'If thou didst know the gift of God and who it is who says to thee, "Give me to drink," thou, perhaps, wouldst have asked of him, and he would have given thee living water.' The woman said to him, 'Sir, thou hast nothing to draw with, and the well is deep. Whence then hast thou living water?'...In answer Jesus said to her, 'Everyone who drinks of this water will thirst again. He, however, who drinks of the water that I will give him shall never thirst.'" (John 4:10–11, 13).

This "gift of God," this "living water," is sanctifying grace with which we receive at baptism the Holy Spirit from the Father and the Son, as Their Gift of Gifts.

But the Son, Who knew what it meant to be thirsty, knew also that we would experience thirst in our body, our mind, our soul. And so He had another name for the Gift of God. This is the sweet name of Paraclete, which means Comforter or Consoler. Sometimes the greatest comfort we know is to cherish a simple gift given long ago by a dear one now departed. You see this when an elderly widow, perhaps having come on hard times, once more has a gleam in her eyes as she proudly points to a bit of bric-a-brac, now painfully dated, saying, "This was a wedding gift."

The Son knew we would have need for a much more solid "consolation." He knew that we would hunger and thirst, suffer and sin. And so He promised to send His Paraclete or Comforter. St. John Chrysostom said, "The Son called Him Paraclete because of the afflictions that then surrounded them" (the disciples). Another appropriate name mentioned by St. Thomas is that of the "complacent joy" of the Father and the Son, since the Holy Spirit is produced by the joyous love which the Father has for the Son. And in this "joy" we share! For in the Divine Family the same love flows from the Father and the Son into the Holy Spirit, whence it ebbs back to its source; ever-flowing again from the three Divine Persons to *us*, only to return again. We, then, become submerged in this veritable inundation of the surging tides of the sole Love within the Godhead. We shall see this more clearly a little later.

We cannot do better, personally, than to address the third Person of the Holy Trinity as Beloved Holy Spirit. "Beloved" spells a sense of belonging. He is eternally breathed forth, to belong to the Father and the Son. He is eternally being sent to belong to *us*.

## Notes

1.    *Summa*, II, Q. 36, Art. 1.
2.    Matthias J. Scheeben, *The Mysteries of Christianity* (St. Louis: Herder, 1946), pp. 75–76.
3.    Tract 105, *De trinitate*, VI, c 5.
4.    Sermon on the Canticle of Canticles, No. 8.
5.    *Op. cit.*, pp. 103–104.
6.    *Op. cit.*, p. 96.
7.    Sermon 23, 16.
8.    *Summa*, II, Q. 38, Art. 2.

# SEVEN

## *Inseparable Family*

T he secret has introduced us to the Persons of the Divine Family. We know Their names. We know Them by "proper" names and "appropriate" names. Thus, Father is the Source and the Unbegotten; Son is Word, Image, or Wisdom; Holy Spirit is Love, Gift, or Paraclete. And names, we recall, bring out the distinction of every "person"—that something by which each one stands out from all others. These appropriate names for the Divine Persons should not seem to us anything unusual. We use appropriate names every day. We often have "nicknames" for our friends, which make for familiarity and often characterize a particular human trait. We also use names that denote some achievement, such as George Washington, Father of His Country; Abraham Lincoln, the Emancipator; Edison, Inventor. But these names, appropriate for Washington, Lincoln, and Edison, we could use for hundreds of other persons who, in common with them, were also founders of countries, emancipators, and inventors.

Surely no one will accuse St. Thomas of being guilty of "anthropomorphism"! But he says that "divine things are named by our intellect...in a way that belongs to things created."[1] And so he justifies our appropriating certain attributes, common to all three Divine Persons, to the Father, Son, or Holy Spirit in particular, for because of our limited capacity they "seem" to belong to one more than to another (just as is the case with certain human personalities). St. Thomas goes on to say:

> For our faith it is fitting that the essential (common to the Three) should be appropriated to the Persons. For although the Trinity of Persons cannot be proved by demonstration, nevertheless it is fitting that it be declared by things which are more known to us...As therefore we make use of the likeness found in creatures for the manifestation of the divine Persons, so also in the same manner do we make use of the essential attributes and such manifestation is called *appropriation*.[2]

St. Thomas gives us this example, quoting St. Hilary: "Eternity is appropriated to the Father; brightness or beauty to the Son; fruition or supreme enjoyment to the Holy Spirit."[3] He explains: Because the "eternal" is not from another source, we call the Father eternal; "beauty" is attributed to the Son, as the perfect Image and Splendor of the Father; "fruition" belongs to the Holy Spirit, since the Father and Son love each other mutually and *enjoy* the Holy Spirit. But we must remember that the Son and Holy Spirit are equally eternal; the Father and Holy Spirit are equally the exemplar of all beauty; the Father and Son are equally fruitful and enjoyable.

St. Thomas also quotes St. Augustine who gives another example of appropriation, as exemplified especially in creatures. Thus, power for the Father, wisdom for the Son, goodness for the Holy Spirit. Why? Again, St. Thomas answers: Because "power" has the nature of principle (source) without principle ("self-propelled"), it is attributed to the Father; "wisdom" has a similarity to the Divine Son (as human son to his father) inasmuch as He is the Word or concept of wisdom; "goodness" is the basis and object of love (human and divine) and thus has a similarity with the Holy Spirit. St. Thomas further adds force to the comparison by noting "dissimilarity" to the weakness in human attributes. Thus, an earthly father grown infirm with age (the Father is eternally powerful); the human son lacks wisdom in his early years (the Son is eternally wise); the human spirit of love can be evil (Divine Love is eternally holy).

You, yourself, use appropriate terms every time you offer Mass with the priest. In the Credo you say: "I believe in one God, the Father almighty, *maker* of heaven and earth" (but the Son and Holy Spirit were equally creators). In the magnificent Preface of the Most Holy Trinity almost every Sunday you say: "It is fitting indeed and just, right and helpful unto salvation for us always and everywhere to give thanks to Thee, O Holy Lord, Father Almighty, Everlasting God."

In this same context St. Thomas says that "these essential attributes are not appropriated to the Persons as if they exclusively belong to Them; but in order to make the Persons manifest." By the same token, Father Scheeben says: "For us who do not behold the Persons in Themselves, this appropriation of activities is almost a necessity, if we are to distinguish the Persons one from another, and are to awaken in ourselves a living interest in each of Them. The fact that the Second Person has in the Incarnation displayed an activity which in a true sense is exclusively His own, increases this necessity. If a special activity were not likewise ascribed to the Father (Creation) and to the Holy Spirit (Sanctification), these two Persons, as far as our view is concerned, would retire to the background."[4]

Appropriating certain attributes and activities to each of the Divine Persons, then, helps to bring out for us Their personalities. But we must recall how They are Persons. The *only* distinctions within the Godhead are fatherhood, sonship, spiration. God is Father because He communicated this same nature to His Son in its entirety; Father and Son pour forth this identical nature into the Holy Spirit. All Three *equally* possess the inexhaustible wealth of divinity. What one is, the others are; what one has, the others have. Everything (save fatherhood, sonship, spiration) They hold in common. We see here "communal" life in its divine ultimate—the divine Exemplar of eternal "co-existence" in the very essence of "peace." Remember, the secret is all about divine life *within* God. The mystery is *multiplicity* in *unity*. That we cannot fathom it only adds to the spell of wonder it casts over us, enticing us on to where we shall see it a little clearer and where we shall live with it forever.

Because of this communal intimacy, this divine co-existence, we say that the Father, Son, and Holy Spirit are "inseparable."

St. Augustine in his Fourth Sermon of Pentecost brings out in a charming, simple way how the members of the Divine Family are inseparable, without losing Their personalities:

> *But the Paraclete, whom the Father will send in My name, He will teach you all things, and bring to your minds, whatsoever I shall have said to you.* Is it that the Son speaks, and the Holy Spirit teaches, so that when the Son speaks we hear the words, and when the Holy Spirit teaches we understand them? As though the Son speaks without the Holy Spirit, or the Holy Spirit teaches without the Son;...the Son also teaches, and the Holy Spirit also speaks, and that when God says or teaches something, it is the Trinity Itself that both speaks and teaches?
>
> But since it is the Trinity, it was necessary to make known Its single Persons, so that we should hear It in Its separate Persons, and understand Them as inseparable. Hear the Father speaking, where you read the words: *The Lord hath said to me: Thou art my son* (Psalms 2:7). Hear again: "No man can come to me, except the Father, who hath sent me, draw him" (John 6:44).

> The whole Trinity therefore both speaks and teaches, but unless It had been made known to us, Person by Person, in no way could the human mind grasp It. Since It is wholly inseparable, if It were always spoken of inseparably, the Trinity would then never be known: for when we speak of the Father and of the Son and of the Holy Spirit, we do not speak of Them together; though They can not be other than together.

In the same Preface of the Mass already mentioned, you profess your faith in this concise, crystal-clear doctrine of the Trinity: "Holy Lord, Father Almighty, Everlasting God, Who together with Thine Only-begotten Son, and the Holy Spirit, art one God, one Lord; not in the singleness of one Person, but in the Trinity of One Substance. For what we believe, by Thy revelation, of Thy glory, the same do we believe of Thy Son, the same of the Holy Spirit without difference or distinction. So that, in confessing the true and everlasting Godhead, distinction in persons, unity in essence, and equality in majesty may be adored."

But no one has put it more simply than the Son. During that final meal with His friends when He told them He was going to prepare a place for them in His Father's house, poor Philip said, "Lord, show us the Father." He must have shaken His head wistfully, for He had already told them: "I and the Father are one" (John 10:30). And so He answered: "Have I been so long a time with you, and you have not known me? Philip, he who sees me sees also the Father.... Dost thou not believe that I am in the Father and the Father in me?" (John 14:9–10). What could be more inseparable than three Persons within one nature?

We have seen how the Word is within the divine mind; how the Son is within the divine bosom; how the Father and Son are within the Person of Their mutual love. All this "withinness" is eternal. There is no departing, no separation. Not only is this true in the inner life of God but also in His outer activities. This is important for us to remember in our thinking about God; in our praying to Him. Too often we address God almost impersonally, that is, vaguely. The only way the Chosen People could address God was as one Person. But *we* know the secret. Why was it revealed to us if God did not want us to make use of it?

With this comprehension our prayer-life will grow in depth when speaking to God the Father, God the Son, God the Holy Spirit, or to the Blessed Trinity of Persons. The Apostles Creed will have a richer meaning for us when, as we profess our faith in each of the Divine Persons in particular, we remember that all Three created us, all Three willed to redeem us, and all Three sanctify us. Our visits to the Blessed Sacrament will be all the more rewarding when we remember that the Son is not alone as we kneel before Him, but that He and we are in the divine company of the Father and the Holy Spirit. Our consolation in receiving the Paraclete will be greater when we remember that we have the consolation not only of a Friend but also of a Father and a Brother. All Three understand us and want to help us.

Sometimes we visit our friends and enjoy them in their delightful intimate family life. When they visit us they often come together, and then we call them inseparable. To be sure, this family "togetherness" gets complicated, so the "victims" of suburbia tell us, especially when they have to reckon with how and when to escape from the children. But there are no complications in visiting and receiving the Family of divine togetherness. In this atmosphere all complications dissolve.

The ancient form of the Gloria Patri was: Glory be to the Father *through* the Son, *in* the Holy Spirit. Amen.

## Notes

1.  *Summa*, II, Q. 39, Art. 2.
2.  *Ibid.*, Q. 39, Art. 7.
3.  *Ibid.*, Q. 39, Art. 8.
4.  Matthias J. Scheeben, *The Mysteries of Christianity* (St. Louis: Herder, 1946), p. 134.

# EIGHT

## *Creative Family*

We have been caught up to the divine atmosphere in the telling of the inner life of God; meeting the Father, Son, and the Person of Their Love. Through divine revelation, our knowledge has been elevated from that of the exterior created world to that of the interior life of God. There is no doubt that this is the mystery of mysteries— the wonder of wonders.

But second to this is the mystery that baffles us almost as much: Why is there any world from which to rise? We might put it another way: Since we have had such a breathtaking flight to the divine plane, let us by a play on words and a wild flight of the imagination picture to ourselves hearing this secret on a plane called heaven, with only the Three and ourselves on board. Being ourselves, we might peek out of the window, and They would understand. Then mortified by our voluntary distraction, as well as confused, we would have to ask: What are all those foamy forms like angel heather (clouds) and those tiny specks way below—red dots (roofs), green needles (trees), blue knots (mountains), beetles (automobiles), ants (men)?

In other words, granting a Family of inexhaustible divine wealth, love, and happiness, what need could They have for such unnecessary trivialities? What need does a millionaire have for a piggy bank of pennies? The answer is: No need. Then why a world? We must repeat the only answer: Love does *even* such things. Love will not stop giving itself. Divine Love is no exception. It is diffusive and seeks to pour itself out to others.

But there were no *others*. Back in eternity which had no beginning there was nothing—absolutely nothing—outside of the Godhead. So the Divine Family took council and decided to *create* something. Such a Family had all that it takes to make something out of nothing, which means, of course, to create. Strictly speaking, the word "creative" belongs exclusively to God. The created creature never creates. He only *makes* things from some already created material. The Divine Family could create because Their divine mind contained millions of creative ideas which Their power could execute, but it was love that moved the divine will to communicate Their divine goodness to the creatable "others" outside Themselves.

And so They made a world—and what a world! We often hear people say: "What a wonderful day, wonderful place, wonderful time, wonderful person!" But who ever bothers to say "What a wonderful world!"? Or, "What a wonderful God Who made it!"? The reason for this is that we seldom see the world as a whole. We are like children who come from a party and remember only how wonderful the ice cream was. They miss the wonder of the party idea and all the fun-making details that made it a success. So we get all excited about the latest astronautic flight, as if there were nothing wonderful to live for now until we can take a trip to Mars, and we exclaim at how much it may cost. Here we can well say with Hamlet: "There are more things in heaven and earth, Horatio, than are dreamt of in your philosophy."

In this very wise reminder, full of practical wisdom for us today, Shakespeare recovers a world full of wonder, practically forgotten in our blasé attitude that it is such a dull place to live—where the weather never suits.

"More things in heaven...." And what is this myth people glibly talk about as heaven? In the first place, it is not an island far out at sea. On the contrary, it is quite in the opposite direction, higher up, figuratively speaking, than the outermost reaches of outer space. And it is part of God's creation. "World" is inadequate to describe what God created. He made a *universe*, and heaven is an essential although not a material part of it. That it is invisible to us does not make it any the less real. It is a segment of the universe that is intimately related to our own material world and our human race.

A human artist leaves the stamp of his personality or the impress of his particular genius on his work. You can always spot a Rembrandt picture, a Duncan

Phyfe piece of furniture, or even a Volkswagen car. So, too, the Divine Family has left Its stamp in the universe. Heaven, earth, and human nature bear witness here. In them you see a created trinity that reflects the Triune Creator. And you see this triple motif repeated throughout the entire canvas of creation; so much so, St. Thomas says, that in all creatures there is found the trace of the Trinity. In every creature are found some things that are necessarily related to one of the Divine Persons. Thus all creatures are created by the power of the Father, the wisdom (divine ideas) of the Son, and the loving goodness of the Holy Spirit. And since St. Bonaventure in his *Journey of the Mind to God* sees all creatures as a "ladder that leads back to God," we learn how practical is the meaning of this triune pattern evident in all creation.

Getting on to the wonders of creation, the Holy Spirit has drawn the veils aside for us in the opening lines of the first recorded history book: "In the beginning God created heaven and earth" (Genesis 1:1). According to St. Thomas, this "heaven" refers not to our firmament of sun, moon, and stars, but to the "empyrean," the fiery or intellectual firmament, not so styled from its heat, but from its splendor; and which was filled with angels immediately.[1] He goes on to say that this heaven is a "corporal" or material place. Just what kind of material, he does not say (naturally, he did not know). All we need to know is that heaven *is* a place—a very definite place, and no mistake about it.

So we meet the angels in their home. And what on earth are angels? Question well put because they are "on earth" a good deal of the time; some of them all the time. Of all God's creatures they are the most forgotten —or worse still, completely unknown. This does not speak very well for such an "enlightened" time as our own. Since we cannot spy on them with supertelescopes or locate them with astronauts, or capture them for scientific experiment, the only practical thing to do is to relegate them to the regions of the purely mythical and forget all about them. All of which means to ignore these masterpieces of creation. If those who deny their existence knew the power they wield on this earth, they would tremble with fear.

Angels are the creatures most like God. They are like Him because they are pure spirits who know and love, possessing their distinct personalities with the most exalted dignity. They are dazzling creatures. Their knowledge sparkles with brilliance. Their love is always at white heat. Their personalities are radiant. Yet compared to God they are as dusty sunbeams to the sun. Compared to us they completely outshine the greatest genius that ever lived. Unlike us they did not receive knowledge the hard way, by laborious study. At the instant of their creation God illuminated their minds with a knowledge of Himself, with the brilliant clarity of His image as in a mirror. In the same instant they received all their knowledge of this world and of ourselves.

The beautiful word "empyrean," from the Greek *pyr*, fire, aptly describes the abode of the angels, who will share it with us eternally. The name indicates the nature of the persons who dwell there. For no light gives the same brilliance and radiance as fire; nothing is more "fiery" than the sun. Where does the charm of candlelight come from but from fire? There are no candles, no stars, in the empyrean—only angel-light. They are reflections not of material but of divine light. They are spiritual images of God Who is Light.

St. Thomas tells us that each angel is not an individual of the angelic species, but that each is a distinct species in himself, the species multiplied in the thousands. "Thousands of thousands ministered to him, and ten thousand times a hundred thousand stood before him" (Daniel 7:10). Each angel reflects, as in spiritual color, refracted rays of the divine light as through a prism, each refraction being a glint of some perfection of God. All the beauties of nature in this world are dull in comparison with these living images of divine beauty, an essential element for beauty being clarity or splendor.

We owe to St. Bonaventure a description of the marvelous resemblance of the Trinity in the angels. He it is who complements the crystal-clear explanation of this mystery by St. Thomas[2] with luminous applications. His writings are saturated with the Trinitarian pattern as seen in creation. In carrying out the "light theme," he says: "God is like a resplendent sun; the Father has the power of this light, the Son the splendor, and the Holy Ghost the warmth, and hence comes the triple illumination of the creature. But as the power of the light shines and warms, its splendor possesses power and warmth, and its warmth possess power and splendor. In the same way we shall be able to contemplate each Person in Himself or in the other Two and from this there will result three illuminations corresponding to the three Persons in Themselves."[3]

The Divine Family showed a fondness for variety and contrast in Their design for creation. We see it repeated constantly. Like all true artists, They achieved beauty through unity amid variety, with the interplay between light and shade. Thus we have day and night, mountains and plains, and the shifting seasons of the year. We have scholars and peasants, rich and poor, big saints and little saints. You may be sure that the idea of a "classless society" does not come out of the mind of God.

This variation theme is not missing in the angelic world. Here we find a fascinating hierarchy of greater and lesser spirits in the harmony of nine angelic choirs. Their names we find recorded in Scripture: Angels or messengers; Archangels, princes or executives for the angels; Principalities, presiding over princes, or leaders of men; Powers, who carry out divine decrees; Virtues, those specially manifesting divine strength or vitality; Dominations, who participate more intimately in the dominion of God in creation; Thrones, picturesque manifestations of God's presence "seated" sturdily within angelic nature; Cherubim, possessing greater fullness of divine knowledge, to be able to communicate this to us; Seraphim, possessing more intense ardor and love for God, in order to enkindle in us greater fervor and contemplation.

It is easy to see from the foregoing how perfectly the angels are related to God as manifestations of His glory; and how the three Divine Persons incorporated them into the Family circle as intimates in the divine council and ambassadors of divine communications. All of which leads to the intimate relation they have to ourselves. The prestige of their "rank" is no barrier to this intimacy. In the divine plan of creation God intended them to be linked with human nature and so there results a strong fraternal bond between us. It is all part of the family idea. We really have much more in common with the angels than with any other of God's creatures. We speak their language—intelligent and spiritual. True, we talk to dogs and canaries, but they do not *understand* us. You will recall that our "conversations" with them are decidedly limited, to say the least.

If you want to discover the importance of the angels and their active interest in mankind, just look through your Bible. There are over three hundred references to them, from Genesis to the Apocalypse, so that, as has been pointed out, you never know when to expect an angel in the Bible. We read: "And when the ass saw the angel standing, she fell under the feet of the rider" (Numbers 22:27). And again: "And the angel of the Lord said to Habacuc: Carry the dinner which thou hast into Babylon to Daniel, who is in the lions' den. And Habacuc said: Lord, I never saw Babylon, nor do I know the den. And the angel of the Lord took him by the top of his head, and carried him by the hair of his head, and set him in Babylon over the den in the force of his spirit.... And the angel of the Lord presently set Habacuc again in his own place" (Daniel 14:33–35, 38).

The angels have no bodies, of course. Being purely spiritual, they have no needs for bodies which would only be a hindrance. As spirits they can move between heaven and earth all the quicker, traveling with the speed of light. Since they cannot be photographed, we have to use our imagination in depicting them. So we give them borrowed costumes for the occasion and picture them in a form which is human but as ethereal as possible, and then add wings to make them different and to accent their swiftness of flight. They really should not object to such cartoon-like representations, because they themselves borrowed human getups many times, as you can read in the Bible. Their appearances, however, were only occasional.

Their chief function is to perform behind the scenes. They enlighten our minds and make use of our imagination. They can make suggestions but can never interfere with the freedom of the will. (Even God respects this freedom.)

Those closest to us are the guardian angels. Their role has been immortalized in one of the most beautiful of the Psalms which is sung at compline, a fitting evening prayer. "He hath given his angels charge over thee; to keep thee in all thy ways" (Psalms 90:11). Here we clearly see the integral part the angels have in our world and the intimate bond with us. No one has put it more touchingly than St. Thomas: "Man while in this state of life is, as it were, on a road by which he should journey towards heaven. On this road man is threatened by many dangers both from within and from without. And therefore as guardians are appointed for men who have to pass by an unsafe road, so an angel guardian is assigned to each man as long as he is a wayfarer. When, however, he arrives at the end of life he no longer has a guardian angel; but in the kingdom he will have an angel to reign with him."[4] And the Angelic Doctor adds a tender afterthought, in saying that in all probability the angel who guards a mother also watches over the child she carries under her heart before it is born, at which time the child receives (its first birthday gift) a guardian angel all its own. This gracious divine gesture of angelic guardians gives us a brief, personal glimpse of the loving providence of the Father, the loving wisdom of the Son, the loving goodness of the Holy Spirit.

In the light of all this, it is positively inconceivable how the angels should ever appear as strangers to us. Besides the fraternal company of our personal angel, how often we meet angels in attendance at the ceremonies of the liturgy! Thus, in the blessing of a new home: "Hear us, O Holy Lord, Father almighty, eternal God, and send Thy holy angel from heaven to watch over, cherish, protect, be with and defend all who live in this house"; in the blessing of an automobile: "Send Thy holy angels to deliver and guard from every danger this car and those who will ride in it"; in the visitation of sick children: "Mercifully grant that as Thy holy angels always minister before Thee in heaven, so by them the life of this child may be protected on earth"; and in the final charge of leading us to heaven: "Command that this soul be taken up by the hold angels and brought home to paradise." In the Mass they play an even more prominent role. Michael the Archangel, together with the saints, receives our confession at the foot of the altar; again we seek his intercession at the incensing of the altar. At the Sanctus we "join with the angels, dominions, powers, and seraphim in singing: Holy, Holy, Holy, Lord God of Hosts." After the Consecration we ask the Father to command an angel (probably Michael) to carry our offering of His Son to "Thine altar on high."

Turning from the empyrean of the angels to this terrestrial world, the mystery of creation unfolds still further. In creating the material part of the universe, the Divine Family surely went in for contrast. As the angels are most like unto God, being purely spiritual, material creation is most unlike Him. The mystery is: how could Divinity make anything so unlike itself? Divine creative power is the answer. Why did God choose this dramatic contrast? It was the divine artistic "instinct," effecting an overwhelming beauty in the universe.

The reason we miss the wonder in the world is because we forget it is a mystery, coming from God; the result is complete confusion and frustration, an enigma. The only key for understanding this mystery is to see it from God's side. Father Walter Farrell, in his *Companion to the Summa*, says it is not the sorrows of life that baffle us with mystery. Original sin explains that; Adam and Eve caused the downpour of grief. Rather it is the joy flooding this world that is the mystery.

Says Father Farrell: "It is not the defects (suffering, vice, ugliness, etc.) that are difficult to explain, but the beauty, joy, perfection, and happiness—the very existence of the universe can be conceived in no other way than as a participation of that divine perfection." All the world is a blueprint of the eternal ideas in the mind of God: the colorful ceremonies of the sun in its rising and its setting, the curving rainbow that smiles through tears, the sparkle in the formal crown of the evening sky; windswept fields with green corn turning gold, kaleidoscopic seascapes, the majesty of mountains; the grace of sea gulls and the liquid tone of larks; the regalness of lions and the playfulness of kittens; the magic spell of music and the living pageantry of flowers and autumn foliage; the charming warmth of firesides and the coziness of homes; the steel in family ties and the cordiality in the love of friends; the tremendous depth in babies and the wisdom of the old; the built-in strength of sorrow and the sweet reward of prayer—all these are ideas from the mind of God.

Regarding the world, man's interest today is splintered. How "old" the world is, and "how" species developed from species are not of primary importance. This is the piecemeal view, breadline stuff. The way to view the world is from mountain-peak heights: whence, why, and then how. This is to see the world as a canvas, not as tiny pieces of a jigsaw puzzle. Incidentally, the "oldest" age date is less than a split second of eternity. But you cannot "process" eternity—you can only deny it.

The current scientific interest in nuclear development fraught with the catastrophic possibility of the very destruction of the world is a case in point of how the marvels of this world can lead away from God's view. There is nothing new about this, of course. It is only the repetition of the old "forbidden-fruit" theme of Paradise. "Creatures of God are turned...to a snare to the feet of the unwise" (Wisdom 14:11). The wise who read aright see every material creature as a sign pointing to the Creator. This is a happy view, the story with the happy beginning and the happy ending—a bit old-fashioned, but it runs safely and yields lots of security. Those who have the key read with St. Paul that "since the creation of the world his invisible attributes are clearly seen—his everlasting power also and divinity—being understood through the things that are made" (Romans 1:20).

Fortunately these are the findings of the queen of sciences, theology, and its applied science of the saints. These keep this view, the only sane view of the world, vigorously alive. Augustine, Thomas, Bonaventure, Duns Scotus, Ignatius and—lest we forget—everybody's Francis of Assisi (with his sister, bird, and brother, wolf), all emphasize that this is a sacramental world, with everything pointing back to God. We hear their echoes throughout the heritage of Christian literature. Shakespeare found "tongues in trees, books in the running brooks, sermons in stones, and good in everything." Did the literary giant steal from the spiritual giant, St. Bernard? "Believe one who knows: you will find something more in woods than in books. Trees and stones will

teach you that which you can never learn from masters"
(*Epistles*, No. 106).

An armchair philosopher put it in a couplet:

> Two men looked out from prison bars,
> One saw mud, the other stars.

The nineteenth-century peer among English poets,
Gerard Manley Hopkins, S.J., amplified this theme to
the dimensions of sheer poetry in his "The Leaden Echo
and the Golden Echo."[5] The first voice despairs at
saving the beauty of God's world:

> "How to keep—is there none such, nowhere
> known,
> some bow or brooch or braid or brace, latch or
> key to keep
> Back beauty, keep it, beauty, beauty, beauty,
> from vanishing away?"

Then the Golden Voice answers:

> "There is one, yes I have one (Hush there!);
> Only not within seeing of the sun
> Somewhere elsewhere there is ah well where!
> One,
> ONE."

Then it gives the golden secret: dedicate the earthly

> beauties of the world to the Creator.
> Resign them, sign them, seal them, send them,
> motion
> them with breath
> And with signs soaring deliver
> Them; beauty-in-the-ghost, deliver it, early now

long before death
Give beauty back, beauty, beauty, beauty, back
to God,
beauty's self and beauty's giver.

What we give to God, then, is in safekeeping.

Not only do we see the label of "Divinity" stamped on every authentic material original in the world, but we see the impress of the creative Family. We see everything as a manifestation of the triple appropriated perfections of the Divine Persons. For everything shows the power of the Father, in its ability to be "functional" (electricity, for example); the wisdom of the Son, in its order (rising and ebbing of the tides to prevent drowning the world); the goodness of the Holy Spirit (letting the seeds develop into potatoes, wheat, and other food).

There is even a similarity between the "production" of the external world and the interior processions of the Trinity. For, we recall, the essential acts of God are knowing and loving. He is then the cause of things by His mind and will, "just as the craftsman by his craft works through the idea (word) conceived in his mind and through the love in his will regarding the object he makes" (St. Thomas). Hence God the Father made creatures through His Word Which is His Son and through His Love, the Holy Spirit. And so, St. Thomas says, the processions of the Persons are the "type" of the productions of creatures which all come from the Father through His knowledge (Son) and love (Holy Spirit).

To complete the triple Family emblem in the masterpiece of creation, the three Divine Persons decided on a happy blend of the spiritual and material that resulted in the making of man. "Let *us* make man to our image and likeness" (Genesis 1:26). Of course, They did not have to go this far. But then, love knows no limits! There just were not enough angels to satisfy the divine outpouring (once They decided to communicate Their love to others). As for the excitement in counting the millions of years in the age of the world, how about starting on the number of the children of men? Much more fun. For this world, no matter how old, was really made for *us* to enjoy. Despite what some people try to make us believe, we are the lords of this material creation. We are not merely of the earth, earthy. Our feet are on the ground, but our heads are erect, eyes gazing toward the empyrean and its citizens who are related to us. "We sense with brutes, but speak with angels" (St. Gregory).

The Holy Spirit had David sing: "What is man that thou art mindful of him? or the son of man that thou visitest him? Thou hast made him a little less than the angels, thou hast crowned him with glory and honour: and has set him over the works of thy hands" (Psalms 8:5–7). Shakespeare knew. He was a Christian. "What a piece of work is a man! how noble in reason! how infinite in faculty! in form and moving how express and admirable! in action how like an angel! in apprehension how like a god! the beauty of the world! the paragon of animals!"

The dignity of man finds accurate expression in Genesis. "And the Lord God formed man of the slime of the earth: and breathed into his face the breath of life, and man became a living soul. And the Lord God had planted a paradise of pleasure from the beginning; wherein he placed man whom he had formed. And the Lord God brought forth of the ground all manner of trees, fair to behold, and pleasant to eat of.... And the Lord God took man, and put him into the paradise of pleasure, to dress it, and to keep it" (Genesis 2:7–9, 15). "And God blessed them [Adam and Eve], saying: Increase and multiply, and fill the earth, and subdue it, and rule over the fishes of the sea, and the fowls of the air, and all living creatures that move upon the earth" (Genesis 1:28).

We do not belong to the animal kingdom—it belongs to us. This is a case of kingdom *above* kingdom. We are to subdue the animals, not to succumb to their level. Somehow the original design of the Creator has gotten horribly blurred in this epoch of confusion! And "creatures *are* turned...to a snare to the feet [and head] of the unwise" (Wisdom 14:11).

This is not to say that we do not share with the animals in the marvelous material fashioned by Divinity in the creation of this world. There is a difference between sharing and identity. St. Francis knew this difference. He took Brother Wolf and his sisters, the birds, into fraternity with himself from his innate sense of reverence for every creature that came from the hand of God. Naturally, he had closer fraternity with and a more sacred reverence for his "Little Brothers," the Friars

Minor. An inner light enabled Francis to gaze on this world with the clarity of extraordinary simplicity, in contrast to the blindness of confusion. "'I praise thee, Father, Lord of heaven and earth, that thou didst hide these things from the wise and prudent, and didst reveal them to little ones'" (Luke 10:21).

We likewise share something with the stones and the trees. Our bodies contain something of all the elements of material nature. With Christian perspective (and reverence) we can examine the human skeleton and see how exquisitely the three Divine Persons covered it with flesh and blood and lots of that purifying, sacred element of water. This is why we call man a microcosm, or little world, in himself. What resembles a miniature world more than man, who not only has a little of everything within his body, but who displays the wonderful order and design of so many intricate details that fit harmoniously in such a tiny enclosure?

But to be human we need more than an animal body. A man acts only because he has a soul. A dead man is dead because his soul has departed. While this is obvious to Christian thinking, the spiritual element in man is considered obsolete in many modern textbooks that flood the market. Animalism has replaced humanity; animality substituting for psychology (study of the soul). This fad has only added more jumble to the confusion, in which the plan has been lost. A man without a soul is merely a skeleton. For the skeleton with flesh and blood add a string, and you have a magnificent puppet

—or, to be in the scientific swing, a mechanical man, a talking animal.

As we saw from the record, God "breathed into his face the breath of life, and *man* became a living *soul*." But what is this soul that exasperates the materialistic scientists because it is intangible? It is the spiritual element that God fused with matter in making up the third segment of His universe. The formula of the Divine Artist for such an effect was, if you will, a blend of the angel and the animal, resulting in the human. If man is a microcosm, he needs light to complete the miniature. In the beginning "the earth was void and empty, and darkness was upon the face of the deep; and the spirit of God moved over the waters. And God said: Be light made. And light was made" (Genesis 1:2–3). So into the "slime of the earth" that was to be man, God breathed the light of life, his soul.

The difference between the light that filled the void of the earth and that which God fused with the material mold of man is the difference between the sun in the sky and the angelic light of the empyrean. In other words, man is a little less than the angels because the mirror of his soul is, as it were, encased in the jewel box of his body, and does not reflect the light of divinity as brilliantly as do the angelic creatures of heaven. Both angels and men are "made to the image and likeness of God"; made to *be* images of God. Man's soul, being spiritual, is akin to God and His angels because it knows and loves.

St. Bonaventure, who sees the stamp of the Triune Artist so constantly throughout the universe, sees it sometimes distinctly, sometimes more faintly; much like an art collector who is now sure in identifying an artist from the distinctiveness of his style or the clarity of his appended name, while at other times he has to study and search. So, he says, it is with the universe. While everything reflects the God Who made it, this reflection is seen, variously, in shadow or in trace or, clearer still, in image. We see the divine shadow in all things being made by God from Whom they have their existence or life. We see the threefold trace in every creature—from the creative power of the Father, the thoughtful wisdom of the Son, and the loving goodness of the Holy Spirit. But it is only in the angels and the souls of men that we see God's image. Angels are like invisible divine stars in the highest heaven; the souls of men are like limpid pools that dot and brighten the land as earth-set stars, reflecting divinity.

St. Thomas sees the image of the Trinity in the light of Divine Providence reflected in our souls. For as the Father conceives His Word, we conceive ideas; as Love flows from Father and Son, love flows from our souls.

St. Augustine sees another resemblance. This illustrious Doctor of the Church was not above speaking as a shepherd to his little flock on a Sunday morning; feeding them not pleasantries but the sublime doctrines of faith, such as the Trinity. With delightful intimacy he puts them at ease as they open their souls to his words. In his Third Sermon for Trinity Sunday he points up the image of the Trinity within our souls, the image of the Three Who are inseparable:

> Whither shall we turn? To the heavens...to the earth? How long, man, will you wander through creation? Turn back to yourself.... Look within yourself to see whether the image of the Trinity may not be there.... Man, have you a memory? If you have not how do you keep in your mind what I have said to you? I wish to know something else. Have you understanding? If you had not a memory, you could not retain what I said. If you had not understanding, you would not know what it was you retained.... I wish to know a third thing. You have a memory by which you retain what is said to you. You have an understanding, by which you grasp what you retain. But as to these two, I ask you: was it not through willing that you both retained and understood? Of course, it was by willing, you will say. You have a will then. These, therefore, are the three things which I undertook to make known to your ears and your minds. These are the three things within you which you can number, but cannot separate. These three: memory, understanding, and will. Observe I say, that these three are made known to us separately and are yet inseparable in operation.

Then, in the human warmth of this saint you can almost see not the Doctor, but the preacher to the people clap his hands in joy: "Thanks be to the Lord our God! He has helped us; He has been near at hand both in you and in me. I declare truly to your Charity that it was with the greatest trepidation that I undertook to discuss and make this known to you. I feared I might please only those with larger understanding, and greatly weary those whose minds are slower. Now I see, as well by the attention with which you listened to me as by the quickness of your understanding, that you have not only grasped what I said, but that you have been ahead of me, in what I was about to say. Thanks be to God!"

What a refreshing lack of confusion on the genius level and the people's level!

## *Notes*

1. *Summa*, II, Q. 61, Art. 4.
2. St. Thomas is called the Angelic Doctor because of his admirable doctrine on the angels.
3. *Hexaemeron*, V, Chap. XXI.
4. *Summa*, II, Q. 113, Art. 4.
5. *Poems of Gerard Manley Hopkins* (London and New York: Oxford University Press, 1956), p. 96.

## *Family Appearances*

The universe created by the Divine Family was not to be one grandiose museum piece that They could gaze down upon. They created, rather, an extension of Their Family that They willed to incorporate intimately with Themselves. The resemblance to the Trinity throughout the universe was to be a family one, not only because it reflected the triune creative Family but also in the sense that children resemble their parents to whom they belong, by family ties and characteristics.

The Divine Family would project into a magnificent exterior the love and bliss of Their interior life, in order to share all this with others; *to share*, not remaining at the far end of an abyss such as exists between a king and his subjects. The sharing would be a union, a wedding between Creator and creatures. The universe would be an outer court in which the Divine Members would mingle intimately with others and communicate the inner riches of divinity.

Unless we see the world from this point of view, it is one huge distortion. It becomes imperative to correct firmly and repeatedly the view of groveling materialists, too much in vogue, who continue to magnify this distortion, overemphasizing excavations of the earth's crust and the bones discovered beneath and giving merely a surface view, to the neglect of the overall picture, and not heeding the exhilarating theme and, above all, the *purpose* of creation.

With feet on *top* of the earth, considered for the moment as the nadir or farthest point, we soar again with St. John in his eagle-flight to the zenith of the Godhead, to read aright the divine plan of this universe. "In the beginning was the Word, and the Word was with God; and the Word was God.... And the Word was made flesh, and dwelt among us. And we saw his glory—glory as of the only-begotten of the Father" (John 1:1, 14).

The phrase "in the beginning" recalls the eternal generation of the Son and reveals the eternal plan of the Father to send His Son "in the fullness of time" into the exterior world. The execution of this plan occurred when "the Word was made flesh." The reason? "For God so loved the world that he gave his only-begotten Son" (John 3:16). We simply cannot get away from St. John's three-word description: "God is love." Love is the theme echoing constantly throughout creation.

Monsignor Romano Guardini, brilliant contemporary theologian, writing on the theme of "the Word was made flesh," under the captivating text from the Book of Wisdom (18:14–15), "For while all things were in quiet silence, and the night was in the midst of her course, thy almighty word leapt down from heaven from thy royal throne," has this to say:

> However, this journey from the everlasting to the transitory, this stride across the border into history, is something no human intellect can altogether grasp.... Before such an unheard-of thought the intellect bogs down. Once at this point a friend gave me a clue that helped my understanding more than any measure of bare reason. He said: "Love does such things!" Again and again these words have come to the rescue when the mind has stopped short at some intellectual impasse. Not that they explain anything to the intelligence; they rouse the heart, enabling it to feel its way into the secrecy of God.[1]

While the Word coming in flesh was the culminating surprise element in the masterpiece of creation, it is at the same time an extension of the Trinitarian life. This stupendous mystery is called the Incarnation, which means a clothing with flesh, another word for body or human nature. But we can never understand the Incarnation without first understanding the significance of the Trinity. The Incarnation flows as an extension of the Trinity. It is this fact that is often overlooked in thinking of the Incarnation.

Many ancient and modern theologians think that the Son would have become Incarnate had Adam never sinned. Thus, Frederic Faber in his work *The Blessed Sacrament*, quoting Rupert, writes: "God created all things because of Christ Who was to be crowned with glory and honor;...all men came because of Christ, not Christ because of them." Others think differently. We are free to believe either view and it is useless to split hairs between pros and cons. Especially is this so if meanwhile it causes us to lose sight of the fuller import that the mystery holds for us.

Probably no one has better brought out this fuller significance of the Incarnation than Father Scheeben, whose *Mysteries of Christianity* has been proclaimed by A. M. Weiss, a renowned Dominican theologian, as "the most original, the most profound and the most brilliant work which recent theology has produced."[2]

Father Scheeben's masterful study, among other valuable insights, gives us a lead that enhances the marvel achieved in creation by the blending of the spiritual with the material in the making of humanity, which we saw in the close of the last chapter. He shows the fitness of human nature for the Son of God.

In the first place, the Incarnation was not necessary for the restoration of the human race to God's favor after sin. God could have forgiven the debt absolutely. He could have sent another Adam. But He chose to send His Son to make perfect, adequate reparation. Suffering was the penalty imposed on the human race because of our First Parents' sin. In the payment God *would suffer*! This sounds almost blasphemous—until we remember *what love does*. Divine nature is incapable of suffering, but it could unite itself to a subject capable of suffering. And so the Father sent His Son into the beautiful world They made, marred only by sin and its consequent suffering, with the result that suffering from then on, tinged with divinity, only added a somber hue to the world's beauty.

Why did not the Son assume an angelical nature? This would be our thought. But God has many better ideas. An angel could not suffer in the flesh, and God *would* suffer. There is a greater reason. "That God's communication of Himself to the outer world may be realized to the full, all created nature must be represented and have a share in it. Created nature is divided into two opposing categories, into spiritual and material nature. In man both elements enter into a union. Man is the microcosm, the world in miniature, his nature is an epitome of the two opposites, the focus in which they are brought together. Therefore if the mission of the Son was to be an introduction into His creation, it had to be directed to human nature as the center of God's external works."[3]

The Roman Martyrology on the Nativity of Our Lord Jesus Christ reads: "The everlasting God and Son of the eternal Father, wishing to consecrate the *world* by His merciful coming, etc." Thus in assuming a human nature the Son embraces the entire universe, lifting it to the level of the Creator. This shows us the vastness implied in the mystery of the Incarnation. This is why no theologian could (or does) say its *sole* motive was reparation.

We must draw from the famous text of St. Paul, "The firstborn of every creature" (Colossians 1:15), as well as cull choice passages from the Fathers, in developing the richness contained in the full import of the Incarnation. First we see the exquisite fitness of human nature itself as the vesture for the appearance of the Son of God. Being the "first-born," Christ is the Head of all creation and of the human race in particular. For while the entire universe comprises a magnificent whole, humanity is unique among the segments in that it has the most perfect oneness of all. Consider, for instance, the prodigious wealth of natural elements, minerals, vegetables, and animals—all fitting into an ensemble of various categories and species. But the human race, for all its accidental differences and numerous members, constitutes a marvelous unity and solidarity. It is not trite but wise (with Christian wisdom) and timely to say that "we are all brothers under the skin," whatever its color.

Basically there is only *one* race, the human race. As we said, another name for humanity is "flesh." So that, speaking grammatically as well as theologically, we say that when "the Word was made flesh" He united His divinity not only to a specific human nature but to the entire race as well. Thus St. Hilary says: "The Son of God assumed the nature of flesh common to all; and having become the true vine, He contains within Himself the entire race of its offspring...that is, He took to Himself the nature of the whole human race."[4]

This does not mean that Christ united His divinity as intimately to our race as to His own sacred humanity, or that we lose our own individuality or autonomy. It does mean, however, that because of His Incarnation

Christ has absorbed to Himself our race, as well as each of us in particular in a very real, concrete manner. "From the whole of human nature, to which was joined divinity, arose, as the first fruit of the common mass, the man who is Christ, by whom *all* mankind was united to divinity."[5]

In thus absorbing to His divinity the totality of our closely knit humanity Christ became the Head of the human race. This added insight of the Incarnation furthers understanding of the recently revived doctrine of the Mystical Body of Christ, which is another name for the Church. While we generally emphasize the necessary incorporation into the Mystical Body through reception of supernatural grace at baptism, this concept of Christ the Son of God assuming human flesh is the foundation of the right of all men to such "deification." By this union in Him we are made sons in Him because He shares our nature and has deified us with His grace.

We also note, in this marvelous fact of the Incarnation, that "even without the Incarnation God could have adopted us as His children and made us brothers of His Son by conferring grace on us directly (as He did with the angels and with Adam and Eve). But without the Incarnation this dignity would have lacked a basis in us and would have been less perfect in its value for us."[6] In other words, God wanted to lift fallen humanity to more exalted heights than it had even before the fall; removing mightily our poverty resultant from the sin of our "first head."

Magnificent, then, is the dignity of every individual, even outside actual participation in the Mystical

Body. Each man, woman, and child demands reverence, at least as a potential member of this Body, because Christ is its Head. We can no more speak of "human cogs" than we can of "square circles" because of the "divinizing" of human nature through the Incarnation. It is not too bold to say that the human race "because of its union with its new head receives an infinite dignity which enables it to discharge *its debt to God* and also to offer Him infinite glorification."[7]

Several of the Fathers crystallize unforgettably this sacredness of human nature flowing from the Incarnation by alluding to the name of the Incarnate Son of God, the Christ, or anointed (indicating the oil, unguent, or chrism used in kingly and priestly consecration; Christ being King and High-Priest of the human race).

St. Peter Chrysologus says: "After the Son of God, like rain falling on fleece, had poured Himself into our flesh with all the ointment of His divinity, He was called Christ, by reason of the unguent. And the sole author of this name is He Who was so flooded and filled with God, that man and God were one God. This name, derived from unguent, He then conferred on us who, after Christ, are called Christians."[8] St. Augustine adds that this "ointment of Christ's divinity" flows over into us "by incorporating us in Himself and making us His members, so that we, too, might be the Anointed."[9]

And St. Leo clarifies for us how Christ's divinity pervades the entire race: "'In Christ dwelleth all the fulness of the Godhead corporally, and you are filled in Him.' The entire divinity fills the entire *body*; and just as nothing is lacking in that majesty by whose habitation the domicile is filled, so there is no part of the body which is not filled with its indweller. But for the statement, 'you are filled in Him,' *our nature* is of course meant, since we would have no share in that repletion unless the Word of God had joined to Himself both a soul and a *body derived from our race.*"[10]

We do not exhaust all that is contained in the Incarnation until we see the divinity of the Son extending to and uniting to itself even the material world, as indicated in the beginning of this chapter. The Incarnate Son of God is the "firstborn of *every* creature." In the words of St. John Damascene: "The gracious will of the Father has effected the salvation of the whole world in His only-begotten Son, and has brought all things together in Him. For, since he is the microcosm, joining in himself every nature, the visible as well as the invisible, the will of the Lord and Creator and Governor of all things ordained that the unity of divinity with humanity, and thereby of every creature, should be accomplished in His only-begotten and consubstantial Son, that thus God might be all in all."[11] The "microcosm" that man is serves as the key word in this beautiful passage. This means that the "unguent" flowing from the head of the Anointed flows over into the beauty and fruitfulness of material creation, giving it the added glint of divinity; demanding the while our reverence as well. Do you now see why St. Francis would "go around" a worm rather than step on it?

St. Paul brings material creation within the scope of the Redemption: "For it has pleased God the

Father that in him all his fullness should dwell, and that through him he should reconcile to himself all things, whether on the earth or in the heavens, making peace through the blood of his cross" (Colossians 1:19–20).

From the microcosm the Incarnation now suddenly whisks us up into the macrocosm, or huge world of the entire universe. St. Paul says specifically that the Son of God, "firstborn of every creature," is also "the head of every *Principality* and *Power*" (Colossians 2:10), meaning the angels. Scheeben also points out that "by His union with humanity the Son of God admits both spiritual and material nature to participation in His divinity; although He thus passes over the angels He does not omit them, since their nature is in a sense comprised in the spiritual element of human nature."[12]

Thus from the wealth of the Scriptures and the inspiration of the Fathers of the Church we learn that we have been highly favored with this mighty cosmic impact of the supernatural mystery of the Incarnation into which we have been intimately incorporated, both our race and ourselves individually; united "member for member" with our Blessed Head.

To dispel the idea that the foregoing explanation of the Incarnation has been too sweeping and that we have lost sight of the central Member of the Divine Family who was supposed to "appear" at this time, we must show you otherwise. The wedding of the Triune Creator with the totality of creatures making up the universe was of gigantic dimensions and implications. The words of the Book of Wisdom imply the same enormous proportions that are packed in that breathless brilliant moment of time when "thy almighty word leapt down from heaven from thy royal throne." But we need more than this.

Before we realize what took place in that tremendous moment, it becomes necessary to listen to a mighty overture elaborating the theme of the Incarnation, with all its overtones. Only then can we hope to understand something of the mystery of the Nativity which telescopes the greater mystery of which it is an "appearance." Should the overture we have assembled from written words be adequately set to music, it would require nothing less than the majestic power of a mighty organ with its thunder—as well as its delicate "vox humana."

We must resort to the saints again (how practical they really are!). St. Bernard, more of heaven than of earth, says: "Indeed I think myself, that the chief reason why the unseen God willed to appear in flesh and mix with men was that He might draw to Himself in flesh the love of those who were not yet able to love save in a carnal manner, and so to lead them gradually on to a spiritual love."[13]

The "golden-tongued" St. John Chrysostom, in a Christmas morning sermon, thus describes the Nativity: He was

> unashamed of the lowliness of our nature. For it was to Him no lowering to put on what He himself had made. Let that handiwork be glorified, which became the cloak of its own

109

Creator. For as in the first creation of flesh, man could not be made before the clay had come into His hand, so neither could this corruptible body be glorified until it had first become the garment of its Maker. What shall I say! And how shall I describe this Birth to you? For this wonder fills me with astonishment. The Ancient Days has become an infant. He who sits upon the sublime and heavenly throne, now lies in a manger. And He who cannot be touched, Who is simple, without complexity, and incorporeal, now lies subject to the hands of men. He who has broken the bonds of sinners, is now bound by an infant's bands. (The last three lines are an insert from St. Cyril of Alexandria).

We find St. John Chrysostom's concept compressed in the paradoxes of a medieval Latin quatrain:

> *Fortitudo infirmitur*
> *Parva fit immensitas*
> *Liberator obligatur*
> *Nascitur aeternitas.*
> As might becomes infirmity
> An infant holds immensity,
> Who comes for liberation
> Is bound by obligation;
> Begotten in eternity
> Is born of virginal-maternity.

How repeatedly, when we hear the haunting Christmas story, ever ancient, ever new, from St. Luke's Gospel, which begins with the decree "that a census of the whole

world should be taken," we think of that Caesar-domi-
nated world and we want to make up for its coldness in
forcing its Maker to be born on one of its neglected outer
edges! It takes another saint to see the mystery within
the mystery in the very words of the Gospel. With saintly
insight Ambrose writes: "While the secular census is
referred to, the spiritual is implied; to be made known,
not to the king of the earth, but to the king of heaven. It
is a profession of faith, an enrollment of souls. That you
may know that census is of Christ, not of Augustus, the
*whole world* is ordered to be enrolled. Who would decree
the enrollment of the whole world, unless He who had
dominion over the whole world? Not of Augustus, but of
the Lord, was it said: "The earth is the Lord's and the fulness thereof"" (Psalms 23:1).[14]

In the Nativity, the Word was silent. His eloquence lay wrapped in infancy—which captured, and
held, and enrolled a world. For thirty years it remained
a "hidden" eloquence, confined to the sacred sanctuary of
a cottage home and the intimates of a (trinitarian)
Family. Then the Word had to be about the business of
His Father, Whom He came to "manifest." At the beginning of His public life the Family that sent Him made a
dramatic "appearance": "Now it came to pass when all
the people had been baptized, Jesus also having been
baptized and being in prayer, that heaven was opened,
and the Holy Spirit descended upon him in bodily form
as a dove, and a voice came from heaven, 'Thou art my
beloved Son, in thee I am well pleased'" (Luke 3:21–22).

St. Augustine, in Sermon 52, on *The Trinity in the Baptism of Christ*, says:

> Here then we have the Trinity brought before us as it were separately: the Father in the voice, the Son in the man, the Holy Spirit in the form of a dove. There was need to bring it to our mind in this way: for to see is the easiest thing to do. For clearly, and beyond any shadow of doubt, the Trinity is here placed before us. Jesus, it says, came; that is, the Son of God. And who can doubt about the dove; or who can say, What does the dove mean, since the Gospel itself tell us most clearly: *The Spirit of God descended upon Him in the form of a dove*? And likewise, who can doubt that it is the Father's voice, since it reads: *This is my beloved Son*? Here then we have the Trinity distinguished one from another.[15]

A "Family Appearance" indeed! But it was not the first. Imagine the startling effect of the Father's voice in this instance. The entire incident was the first telling of the secret—told in a human voice. What more fitting medium of "appearance" for the Father than a voice? "One can say that there is no emotion either of happiness or sadness, tenderness or violence, which is not reflected in the voice, as the orator, singer, actor, or professor well knows. Each of these makes competent use of the voice."[16] And what is more indicative of fatherliness than the voice? This is the human instrument that conveys to the family protective authority, decisions, encouragement, and good order—all with overtones of strong fatherly love. How tender and fatherly a gesture this, to communicate the secret directly by voice, man, and dove! Incomprehensible Divinity accommodating Itself to the simplicity of human eyes and ears!

While St. Matthew records the voice saying, "This is my beloved Son," Sts. Mark and Luke have it, "Thou art my beloved Son." Cornelius à Lapide in his classic commentary on the Scriptures indicates that this latter rendering is consistent with the entire context of the incident of the Baptism, because "Jesus gazing into Heaven was praying to His Father, and as the Holy Spirit descended on Him, the Father's voice was directed to Him, encircled and joined Him, as *His Son*, so that He would be set before the whole world to be venerated, loved and heard."[17] In other words, this Family meeting and intimate conversation in Their external world projected the harmonious union existing in the sanctuary of Their inner life—all centering in "My beloved Son."

Why the dove? The dove has ever been a symbol of peace, gentleness, and love. We find hundreds of such references from the dawn of history, down through pre-Christian times to our own day. It was the dove that brought back to Noah an olive branch, indicating that God had let the waters subside after the Flood. (Doves have acted as messengers ever since.) Christ told the apostles to be "simple as doves."

> The dove is the loveliest and most striking
> symbol of the Holy Spirit. Its form and color
> put us in mind of the grace and purity of the
> Holy Spirit. Its rapid but unagitated flight

represents His lively yet controlled emotion. Its low murmur is like the expression of love which we have come to associate with the Holy Spirit. Following the baptism in the Jordan, the dove hovered between the Father and His Incarnate Son, descending from the former to the latter. Thus in eternity, in virtue of His relation to the Father and the Son, the Holy Spirit hovers between them; He shelters them, as it were, under His wings, and brings them together in Himself in blissful embrace, crowning and perfecting their love.[18]

Again, "the dove is the gentlest, simplest of birds; the most innocent, fruitful, ardent, and selfless" (feeding the brood of other birds).[19]

On the second occasion when the Divine Family appeared together, on the top of Mount Tabor, at the Transfiguration, the voice addressed the privileged apostles Peter and James and John directly (to encourage them): "As he was still speaking, behold, a bright cloud overshadowed them, and behold, a voice out of the cloud said: "This is my beloved Son, in whom I am well pleased; hear him'" (Matthew 17:5).

Here again is the Fatherly voice in practically the same words speaking about His beloved Son. "'Hear him,' that is to say, Hear Christ, who is my only-begotten; not Plato, nor Apollo, nor Socrates; Christ, I say; hear and believe in Him; He, from my bosom, will announce to you secrets, hidden from the foundation of the world."[20] The "man" appears, not in the humble role of a baptized penitent, but in subdued glory, for "his face shone as the sun, and his garments became white as snow" (Matthew 17:2). And in place of the spreading wings of the divine dove, the Holy Spirit encircled the Two in a "bright cloud."[21]

When the Father's voice is heard a third time, it is alone, and to comfort His Son, in response to His words: "'Now my soul is troubled. And what shall I say? Father, save me from this hour! No, this is why I came to this hour. Father glorify thy name!' There came therefore a voice from heaven, 'I have glorified it, and I will glorify it again.' Then the crowd which was standing round and had heard, said that it had thundered. Others said, 'An angel has spoke to him.' Jesus answered and said, 'Not for me did this voice come, but for you.'" (John 12:27–30).

The other visible appearance of the Holy Spirit, alone, was in flame and wind, on Pentecost. Here, in contrast to the "Spirit breathing where it will," like a zephyr, silently within the soul, we hear the roaring of a "mighty wind" symbolizing the power of Love that can sweep men into the orbit of divinity. Here the brightness of the cloud is intensified to the heat of the fire (that would enkindle but not burn) as the Holy Spirit hovers in flaming tongues over the apostles, to dramatize the divine eloquence He forged in their souls. In contrast to the gentle brooding of a dove, we have fire-dipped tongues that will proclaim this man as the Son of God, through human words to human ears.

These appearances of the Father and the Holy Spirit—on the auspicious occasions of the Son's formal beginning of His "Father's business," on the heights of Tabor, about six days after the prediction of the Passion, to dispel the "scandal of the cross," and again on the birthday of the Church—all served to highlight the appearance of the Incarnate Son. They enhanced His prestige and confirmed His mission, in a visible manner, before the sight and hearing of men. But more significantly, they manifested externally the inseparable, yet distinct, Members of the Divine Family. They manifested openly the intimate divine fellowship, never absent invisibly, from the time the Son of God appeared at Birth, as He walked through Palestine, and until He finally expired on Calvary.

As already mentioned, the Incarnation is a prolongation of the Trinity. If we see the Trinitarian pattern in every stick and stone, in every bird and beast, in every angel and man, would we expect it to be missing in the created masterpiece, par excellence, that integrates the entire universe to Himself—the Incarnate Son? This is not a "pattern" extended or repeated; rather is it the externalizing of the unique interior processions of the eternal begetting of the Son and the mutual breathing-forth of Their common Love. Life in the divine bosom flows over into all creation, flooding and absorbing it—in the flesh of the Son, Who is the same focal point in creation as He is in the inner life.

Hence it is that Christ the Son of God is the "firstborn" of creatures, in time, as He is generated within the Godhead eternally. His chief "business" is to manifest the Father in the universe. Recall His words to

Phillip: "He that seeth me seeth the Father also. Do you not believe that I am in the Father and the Father in me?" Recall also His references to the Father; recall His repeated promises to send "another" Paraclete (inseparably united to Him and the Father).

The Gospel is referred to as a full development of the Divine Trinity because this was the sum and substance of the "Father's business." Christ perfectly summed up the purpose of His appearance in the world in the "triple" name He gave Himself: "I am the way, and the truth, and the life. No one comes to the Father but through me" (John 14:6).

Every truth He taught was manifestation of the divine mind of which He was the eternal as well as the incarnate spokesman. The way He taught and exemplified could lead only to the Father. The life was none other than that eternally lived in the bosom of the Divine Family. The crowning peak of His teaching concerned this divine life; this was the ultimate goal of the way; this the essence of the "kingdom" He came to give away in an extravagant manner. "I came that they may have life, and have it more abundantly" (John 10:10).

Incarnate "Spirit," He communicated not only divine knowledge but divine love to other created spirits who could understand and love in return, as "deep calleth on deep" (Psalms 41:8).

"Greater love than this no one has, that one lay down his life for his friends" (John 15:13). It was for the Son to prove the measure of the "greater love" of the divine in human terms. As the Son's initial eloquence was in the silence of infancy, the climax of this eloquence was in stillness, the stillness of death. The Word became wordless in His most eloquent moment, for on Calvary divine love became a flaming sign "nailed up" in a dead body.

## Notes

1.      Romano Guardini, *The Lord* (Chicago: Regnery, 1954), p. 15.
2.      Translator's Preface. Emile Mersch, S.J., in his *The Whole Christ* (Milwaukee: Bruce, 1936) brings out many of the same insights of the Incarnation, but more specifically as related to the Mystical Body, drawing copiously from the Fathers, as does Father Scheeben whose scope extends to the nine key mysteries of Christianity.
3.      Matthias J. Scheeben, *The Mysteries of Christianity* (St. Louis: Herder, 1946), p. 362.
4.      St. Hilary of Poitiers, *Commentary on Psalm 51*.
5.      St. Gregory of Nyssa, *Commentary on 1st Corinthians*.
6.      Scheeben, *op. cit.*, p. 382.
7.      *Ibid.*, p. 354.
8.      *Homily 60*, in PL, LII, 367.
9.      *Commentary on Psalm 26*.
10.    *Sermon 10 on the Nativity of Our Lord*.
11.    *Homily on the Transfiguration of Our Lord*, No. 18.
12.    Scheeben, *op. cit.*, p. 363.
13.    *Sermon on the Canticle of Canticles*, No. 20.
14.    Quoted in *Catena Aurea*.
15.    In a Note on page 83 of *The Sunday Sermons of the Great Fathers*, translated and edited by Rev. M. F. Toal, D.D. (Chicago: Regnery, 1959), it is stated: "This is one of the most significant sermons ever delivered. It is also a masterpiece of the didactic art; making clear, exact, precise (and human), a theme of the utmost sublimity, and while at the same time arousing (and holding) interest and attention, and, it would seem, clamorous appreciation."

16.  Pius XII, Allocution to the Otorhino-larynology Society, 1959.
17.  Cornelius à Lapide, *Commentary on Matthew, Chapter 3, Verse 17.*
18.  Scheeben, *op. cit.*, p. 154, ftn.
19.  Tertullian, *On the Incarnation*, Chap. 3.
20.  Cornelius à Lapide, *op. cit.*
21.  Origen, *Commentary on John 5:37.*

# TEN

## *Mother in the Family*

We have seen the tremendous scope and impact of the Incarnation. What more could possibly remain for us to consider in regard to it? Precisely this: How did this creative prodigy take place? In answer to that question lies a world in itself. And the name of this world is Mary.

The Divine Family presented the Incarnation to us in an envelope. Mary was that envelope. The story of the Divine Family contains mystery within mystery. And here we have another mysterious divine paradox. As Mary was the envelope that contained the Incarnate Son of God (while necessarily containing the Father and the Holy Spirit), the Divine Family, at the same time, was an "envelope" that fully contained Mary, whom Gabriel saluted thus: "Hail, full of grace." This fulness of grace was the flooding of Mary's soul with the Triune Presence and life of divinity to a degree that surpassed the measure of the "abundant life" of all the millions of angels and men that ever existed or ever would exist—all taken together.

When we speak about Mary we are unmistakably in another world, but a world that is no more remote from ourselves than is any mother from her child. Here is the world of the Incarnation—of the God Who united Himself to all men. And she stands in its center with the Son to Whom she gave flesh of her flesh. Mary envelopes the Trinity, especially the Son, and the Trinity envelopes Mary in a unique manner, because of the role They eternally decreed she should play in the Incarnation of the Son, the redemption of the world, and the sanctification of men.

If to see the world aright is to see it from the divine mind that planned and executed it, then to understand the Incarnation completely is to understand the divine plan in which it was conceived. Mary is so essential to that plan that its fulfillment depended on her acceptance. Tradition, from St. Justin (A.D. 165) and St. Irenaeus (A.D. 203) down to our own day has attached enormous importance to Mary's *Fiat*, or acceptance: "Be it done to me according to thy word" (Luke 1:38). As St. Bernard puts it:

> The Angel awaits the answer, for the moment is at hand when he must return to God who sent him. And we, too, O Queen, are awaiting the word of compassion, we who are weighed down with the sentence of damnation, leaving us wretched. Behold the price of our salvation is being offered to you; if you give your consent, we shall be freed at once. By your brief

answer we are to be re-created, so as to be
restored to life. This, O loving Virgin, this,
Adam in his sorrow entreats of you...this,
Abraham and David, too, implore. This also
the holy men of old, your ancestors no less,
earnestly beg, they themselves who dwell in
the valley of the shadow of death. This, in
fact, the whole world on bended knee before
you is awaiting...O Virgin, give your answer
quickly. Speak, O Queen, speak the word
which the living on earth, the dead below, and
the angels above, all are awaiting.[1]

The Divine Family decreed that the Incarnate Son
should have a mother. Why not? For what is more *human*
than to have a mother? And never was any mother in the
history of the world as famous as the one named Mary.
Her fame, all her dazzling titles and the totality of divine
wealth lavished on her as a dowry for the marriage of
her Son with humanity owe their foundation to her
motherhood.

What the villagers of Nazareth and Bethlehem
missed was this: the fragile fifteen-year-old peasant wife,
expecting her child, was the woman featured in the opening chapter of the Scriptures; the same valiant woman
who would be seen in the final book narrating the
prophetic vision of the heavenly Jerusalem. Nothing less
than the inspired word of God has placed Mary immor-
tally where she belongs. So there would be no mistake,
God "wrote" her into His plan. No power in heaven, in
hell, or on earth can displace her—"constant as the

northern star, / of whose true-fix'd and resting quality / There is no fellow in the firmament."[2]

Thus in Genesis we read of her power: "I will put enmities between thee and the *woman*, and thy seed and her seed: she shall crush thy head, and thou shalt lie in wait for her heel" (Genesis 3:15). In the Apocalypse we see her radiant beauty: "And a great sign appeared in heaven: a *woman* clothed with the sun, and the moon was under her feet, and upon her head a crown of twelve stars" (Apocalypse 12:1). Halfway in the Bible is the Canticle of Canticles, the Song of Songs, which sings of both her beauty and her power in one majestic verse: "Who is she that cometh forth as the morning rising, fair as the moon, bright as the sun, terrible as an army set in array?" (Canticle 6:9).

Mention of Mary in Scripture is at a minimum, as befits the humility she always wore as a priceless jewel. With motherly (and queenly) dignity she played her powerful role in the background. The brevity of references to her serves all the better as brilliant highlights, compelling conspicuous recognition. What is recorded is always significant.

It is with divine delicacy that the Holy Spirit inspires St. John, alone, to see Mary as Queen-Mother in glory in his vision. Who had a greater right than the "favorite disciple"? Among the evangelists, it was he alone who introduced her at the wedding feast in Cana, on the occasion of the first miracle, performed by Christ at the request of His Mother. It is to St. John that we owe this scriptural reference to the "power of the Blessed Virgin's intercession and even the law of her mediation."[3]

As it was John who always saw more the divine than the human in the Son of God, it was he who received the plan of the Incarnation personally, in its entirety, including the divine maternity. His reward for not running away at the bitter end, on Calvary, was the precious gift of Mary for his mother. There was nothing more to give! At the last, Christ gave the best—second to Himself. To Mary standing at the foot of the Cross He said, "'Woman, behold thy son.' Then he said to the disciple, 'Behold thy mother'" (John 19:26–27). What a beggarly substitute this was for Mary! (Did the sword turn at this point—for, after all, her motherly heart was human?)

But it must have been only seconds after this double bequest that, as if in a flash of lightning, John knew his gift was not really personal; he became a recipient for the race. In the same instant Mary realized she was doubly a mother—her children coextensive with all humanity. She would not lose her Son, but would keep Him in extended incarnations. John, too, saw the divine in the plan. St. Pius X, quoting St. Augustine and St. Grignon de Montfort, clearly brings out this extended motherhood of Mary:

> Is not Mary the Mother of Christ? Therefore she is also our Mother.... Now as the God-man He received a real, material body, like other men; but as the restorer of our race He possesses a body that is, so to speak, *spiritual*

and, as they say, *mystical*, this body consisting in those who believe in Christ. "The many, are one body in Christ" (Romans 12:5). The Virgin conceived the eternal Son of God not only so that He might become man, receiving from her His human nature, but also that through the nature received from her He might be the Savior.

Thus, in one and the same womb of His most chaste Mother, Christ both took His human flesh and joined to it a spiritual body, consisting of those who were to believe in Him. Accordingly, Mary *who bore the Savior in her womb, can also be said to have borne all those whose life was contained in the life of the Savior.* Hence all of us who are united with Christ, in other words, all who, as the Apostle says, "are members of his body, made from his flesh and from his bones" (Ephesians 5:30), all, I say, came from the womb of Mary, being joined to the head, as it were, in the manner of a body. *Hence, in this spiritual and mystical manner we are called the sons of Mary and she is the Mother of us all.*[4]

This extended motherhood of Mary, which includes all of us—her "other Christs"—echoes eternally in the crystal-clear words of her dying Son: "Behold thy mother." Such was His will, such His plan. Mary accepted this plan in her original *Fiat* at Nazareth which, never revoked, carried over to Calvary. She consented to every detail involved. "The origin of Mary's glories, the solemn moment which lights up her whole personality and *mis-*

*sion*, is that in which she, being full of grace, replied to the Archangel Gabriel with the *'Fiat'* (Be it done), expressing her consent to God's plan."[5] "When she uttered her *Fiat* at Nazareth and again on Calvary, she conceived us all and gave us birth."[6]

Thus the entire pattern of the Incarnation is consistent throughout—Mary giving birth without pain at Bethlehem, but enduring pain at the blood-drenched birth under the Cross. The *Fiat* of the Annunciation attains full bloom at the redemption—the virgin-white rose of Nazareth becomes the ruddy "first rose of martyrs"[7] at Golgotha.

Mary's suffering on Calvary fulfilled the prophecy uttered by Simeon at the presentation of Christ in the Temple: "And thy own soul a sword shall pierce" (Luke 2:35). Christ gave her the title and role of Mother of men in virtue of His will, but also because she merited these (through charity and suffering) by her intimate union with His own Passion. Hence the Fathers have called her *socia Passionis*, or companion of the Passion. Of this relationship between Mary's suffering and motherhood, Pope Pius XII in his encyclical on the Mystical Body wrote: "She it was who...ever most closely united with her Son, offered Him on Golgotha to the Eternal Father, together with the holocaust of her maternal rights and motherly love, like a new Eve, for all the children of Adam contaminated through his unhappy fall, and thus she who was the mother of our Head according to the flesh became by a new title of sorrow and glory the spiritual mother of all its members."

From Mary's spiritual motherhood of men, resulting from her *Fiat* at the Cross, blossomed added titles and added "involvement"—all contained within the plan of the Incarnation. Thus Mary is rightly called the co-redeemer, mediatrix, and dispenser of all the graces stemming from the redemption. On this point there is some discussion, not so much as to the three respective roles of Mary, but rather as to the manner in which she performs them.

Cardinal Suenens, already quoted, admirably clarifies this issue in *Mary the Mother of God*: "True devotion to Mary takes its rise not from below but from above: not from feelings of affection but from faith. In the first place it means clinging to God and accepting his design.... God has willed to associate Mary with his work of salvation.... It is not for us to set limits to the divine action or to dispense with the intermediaries which God has freely chosen.... In God there is room for every kind of superabundance, and it is only at our level that restriction or niggardliness is to be found."[8]

In the sixth and ninth chapters of this work, the Cardinal gives the interpretation of the Church regarding the titles of co-redemptrix and mediatrix: "Our Lady's cooperation in the sacrifice of the cross has received the particular name of co-redemption. Is it or is it not, fitting that she should be designated the *Co-redemptrix?*... It belongs to the Church to fix the language of her theology, and to judge whether or no any confusion is likely to occur in certain cases; and in authorized documents the *magisterium* [teaching office] of the Church tends increasingly to favour the expression *Co-redemptrix* to express this doctrine. It has now received the 'freedom of the city,' so to speak, and it remains for us to explain what it involves."[9]

We read further:

Therefore the Church teaches the doctrine of Mary's mediation in the present. Is this dogma of faith? No, but it is a truth of faith admitted and recognized by the ordinary *magisterium* of the Church, and as such proposed to us.

> There is a tendency at the present day to allege that a doctrine is neither certain nor revealed until it has been solemnly defined either by the pope speaking *ex cathedra* or by a General Council in union with him. We must not think that only truths thus defined are proposed to us as absolutely certain. Such an attitude was expressly condemned in the *Syllabus*, which rejects the proposition that 'the strict obligation which binds Catholic teachers and writers is limited to the statements proposed to the faithful, to be believed by all, as dogmas of faith by an infallible decision of the Church.' Furthermore, the Vatican Council explicitly recognizes a twofold teaching of the Church, that which is given by way of solemn definition and that imparted by way of her ordinary *magisterium*: that is, the teaching which she gives to her children by her normal, daily instruction. This latter teaching can be gathered from the documents addressed by the Holy See to the universal

Church, from the pastoral letters of the bishops, from the catechisms which are the expression of the common instruction of the Church, and also from the prayers of the liturgy in universal use, according to the saying, *Lex orandi est lex credendi*: as is the prayer, so is the belief.

In his Encyclical *Humani Generis*, Pius XII reminded us that the authentic interpretation of the revealed deposit of faith is entrusted to the *magisterium* alone, "which carries out this duty, as has often happened in the course of the centuries, either by the ordinary or extraordinary exercise of that power."

If we bear these principles in mind, we must conclude that the mediation of our Lady comes within the *magisterium* and therefore requires our acceptance. It is not requisite that it should be defined as a dogma binding on all Catholics, and it belongs to the Church alone to judge as to the opportuneness of a definition which hitherto she has not considered necessary.[10]

Precisely what do the titles Co-redemptrix and Mediatrix mean and imply? To answer, we need to explain the role of Christ the redeemer and mediator. Our Lord redeemed all men. That is, He "bought back" a fallen humanity, restoring it to divine favor. He paid the price of our sin incurred through Adam. "You know that you were redeemed...not with perishable things, with silver or gold, but with the precious blood of Christ" (1 Peter 1:18–19).

"For you have been bought at a great price" (1 Corinthians 6:20).

The role of redeemer included that of mediator. That is to say, as Christ "paid the price" for our sinfulness, He at the same time reconciled us to the Father and earned for all men the right to receive graces which would effect this reconciliation, in making us children of God. He was the medium between the Father and us, the divine "go-between." In thus reconciling us He interceded for those necessary graces. To mediate means to effect a reconciliation by acting as an intercessor. The application or distribution of these graces was to take effect, individually, through sacramental contact in baptism and the other sacraments.

Obviously, the redemption by Christ was infinitely adequate for all men. "For there is one God, and one Mediator between God and men, himself man, Christ Jesus, who gave himself a ransom for all" (1 Timothy 2:5–6). But it was His will that He incorporate others in His mediation. Otherwise how could St. Paul say: "What is lacking of the sufferings of Christ I fill up in my flesh for his body, which is the Church" (Colossians 1:24)? And what are the saints, whose intercession we implore, if not lesser mediators? But it was the divine will that Mary enjoy a unique union with her Son in such intimacy that she becomes, as St. Thomas says, "mediatrix with the Mediator." And Pius XII echoes the same: "She too it was who by her most powerful intercession obtained for the newborn Church the prodigious Pentecostal outpouring of that Spirit of the divine Redeemer who had already been given on the cross. She, finally, true queen of martyrs, by bearing with courageous and confident heart her immense weight of sorrows, more than all Christians 'filled up those things that are wanting of the sufferings of Christ for his body, which is the Church.'"[11]

We must clearly understand that Mary's capacity as co-redemptress and mediatrix is entirely subordinated to that of Christ. There is no question here of equal collaboration, naturally. In no way is she independent of the results of the redemption; she being, in fact, the first-fruit of the redeeming act, by anticipation, in her glorious privilege of the Immaculate Conception. So, too, her mediation is subordinated to Christ's. She is a mediatrix under Him. In other words, the Son willed to integrate and incorporate with His own her suffering, given generously and freely at the Incarnation and the Crucifixion.

This mutual redemption and mediation, taking place on Calvary, gave men the right to graces necessary for salvation. The actual acquisition and distribution of such graces take place individually in the here and now. Because of this fact, when we think of Mary as mediatrix we generally associate her power of intercession with our present needs. "All graces merited by Christ come to us through Mary," as we say. You see, Mary's motherhood was not to cease at giving birth to the Mystical Body. It is the nature of motherhood to nurture the growth of children from birth to maturity and to continue this motherly influence thereafter. Mary was no exception. So it was in the plan that she be associated with Christ, not only at Bethlehem and Calvary, but also at the Pentecost of the Cenacle and all the pentecostal moments from then to the end of time, into eternity. "Holy Mary, pray for us *now* and at the hour of our *death*."

The only area of theological discussion on this point lies in the manner of this distribution of graces that contribute to our spiritual growth, coming from Christ through the hands of His Mother. Some say her mediation is limited to that of "pure prayer," while others hold that it "involves a more direct influence, although such is always derived from and subordinated to the unique mediation of Christ."[12]

Can we not say, then, that Mary's titles of co-redemptrix and mediatrix stand forth like twin towers of an impregnable fortress, as a background for her who is called "terrible as an army set in array"? We find these titles buttressed by the weight of early Tradition and down through the centuries, from the writings of the Fathers to the official pronouncements of recent popes. Like the pealing of a carillon we hear: "A virgin is instrumental in saving the human race" (Irenaeus, 203); "All sanctity was, is, and ever shall be derived from Mary" (St. Ephraem, 373); "Through Mary every faithful spirit is saved" (St. Cyril of Alexandria, 444); "Through Mary we have received a remission of our sins" (St. Modestus, Patriarch of Jerusalem, seventh century); "It is the will of God that we receive all things through the hands of Mary" (St. Bernard, 1153); "...dispenser of all graces" (Pius VII); "Why should He not use His mother's office and efforts to bring us the fruits of the redemption?" (Pius IX); "She merited to become in a most worthy manner the restorer of the world, and thereby the distributress of all blessings that Jesus through His blood and death acquired for us" (St. Pius X); "...that together with Christ she redeemed the human race" (Benedict XV); "Thou who as co-redemptress was filled with compassion as thou stoodst at the side of thy most dearly beloved Son..." (Pius XI); "As mother and co-operatrix, she remains forever associated to Him, with an almost unlimited power, in the distribution of graces which flow from the redemption" (Pius XII).

The last-quoted Pontiff, of blessed memory, added to the luster of Mary's crown of titles, toward the close of the Marian Year of 1954, significantly enough on the Feast of her Motherhood, October 11th, by solemnly proclaiming the Feast of her Queenship over the entire universe of heaven and earth. In the encyclical letter of proclamation he graciously recognizes the humble, yet powerful, role of all Mary's children, in perpetuating the sacred tradition of the Church concerning their mother, and including her queenship, from the earliest times of the Catacombs when they traced her picture as the chief *orante* or praying figure, with arms upstretched, and not passing over the "crown of roses" they constantly finger today, in the intertwining mysteries of Jesus and Mary from the Annunciation through the *Via Crucis* to the crowning of their queen.

This saintly father of Christendom closes his letter thus:

> Therefore from the monuments of Christian antiquity, from the liturgical prayers, from

the Christian people's profound sense of religion, and from the works of art that have been produced, We have collected statements asserting that the Virgin Mother of God possesses royal dignity. Likewise We have proved that the arguments which sacred theology has constructed by reasoning from the deposit of faith completely confirmed the same truth. From so many testimonies gathered together there is formed, as it were, a far-sounding chorus that praises the high eminence of the royal honor of the Mother of God and men, to whom all created things are subject and who is "exalted above the choirs of the angels unto heavenly kingdoms."

In the following month, on November 1st, Feast of All Saints, Pope Pius XII personally crowned the famous painting *Salus Populi Romani*, temporarily removed from its place in the Basilica of St. Mary Major to a prominent square in the city. This gesture, honoring the Queen of Saints, often performed by many of his predecessors, confirmed with papal prestige the traditional practice of Mary's children of all ages and ranks who love to honor their Mother with continual crownings. For the occasion he recited the special prayer in harmony with the new feast:

> Reign over men's minds that they may seek
> what is true; over their wills that they may
> follow solely what is good; over their hearts

that they may love nothing but what you yourself love.

Reign over individuals and families, as well as over societies and nations; over the assemblies of the powerful, the counsels of the wise, as over the simple aspirations of the humble.

Reign in the streets and squares, in the cities and the villages, in the valleys and the mountains, in the air, on land and on sea; and hear the pious prayer of all those who recognize that yours is a reign of mercy, in which every petition is heard, every sorrow comforted, every misfortune relieved, every infirmity healed, and in which, at a gesture from your gentle hands, from death itself there arises a smiling life.

Obtain for us that all who now, in every corner of the world, acclaim and hail you Queen and Mistress, may one day in heaven enjoy the fullness of your kingdom in the vision of your Divine Son, Who with the Father and the Holy Spirit lives and reigns for ever and ever Amen.

The closing of this prayer with the hope of enjoying the fullness of Mary's kingdom in the vision of her Son, "with the Father and the Holy Spirit," reminds us that we never really see Mary completely until we see her in the Trinity. Remember it is the Trinity that holds the universe together. And of all, Mary is the most precious creature upon which They gaze. The role of prolific motherhood which this Divine Family eternally destined for her became a reality in the instant of the Incarnation. She was the first to hear the secret, personally. The sublime invitation to be the Mother of God came in the name of the Triune God: "The *Holy Spirit* shall come upon thee and the power of the *Most High* shall overshadow thee; and therefore the Holy One to be born shall be called the *Son of God*" (Luke 1:35). "The work of the conception was common to the whole Trinity, yet in some way it is attributed to each Person.... The Most High is the Father, whose power is the Son."[13] Some, with Cornelius à Lapide, attribute "Most High" to the Holy Spirit.

The words "full of grace" indicated the prodigious degree of Mary's participation in that divine nature that is undivided and common to the Father, Son, and Holy Spirit. Unique among all others ("blessed art thou among women," that is, all creatures), she is a magnet who drew the Trinity to herself. (They made her for that purpose.) She is likewise a magnet drawing us to the Trinity. This is her role; a magnet, if you will, having a twofold power of attraction.

This is all part of the "why" of the Incarnation. Why did the Son become incarnate if not to lead us to the Father in union with the "other Paraclete"? This is the why of the Father's twofold sendings. And this is the why of Mary. It all goes back to the eternal flowing and ebbing within the Trinity, from the Father to the Son and Holy Spirit, back to the Fatherly bosom; and the overflowing of this divine life into created humanity from the Source, by the Word, through Love—and, by Their choice, through the channel called Mary. But this overflowing was for the sole purpose of an ebbing return. In the plan, Mary leads back to the Trinity. In the litany do we not invoke her (theologically) as *Janua Caeli*, Gate of Heaven? And again, as *Mater Divinae Gratiae,* Mother of Divine Grace?

Mary, then, is mother, co-redemptress, mediatrix, dispenser, queen, that she might be the gate through which we enter into the "blessed vision of peace" (Beatific Vision of the Trinity) in a "house not made with hands" and attain the fulfillment of the heavenly destiny for which we were created.

It is within the trinitarian focus that we must also see this other supremely significant facet of her motherly relation to the Son, namely, her presenting Him to the world and her leading the world to Him. Who, but she, presented Him, already incarnate, to his cousin St. John who on this occasion leaped with joy, even before he was born? Who, but she, presented Him at the court of the cave at the Nativity and the Epiphany? And was it not she that presented him formally and publicly to the world in the temple?

But it is in conjunction with her present role as mediatrix before the throne that she leads us to Christ. If it is the Triune will that she dispense sharings in the divine life she cooperated in meriting with the Son, it is necessarily in accord with the same divine will that we seek these graces from her. Else for what purpose a God-given co-mediator? But always, in the words of St. Thomas, mediatrix *with* the Mediator, noting furthermore that "properly speaking, the office of a mediator is to join together those between whom he mediates."[14] With this phrase in mind, there is no fear of "displacing" Christ, no fear of "interference," in not going to Christ directly. Such absurd fear is groundless. Mary as a magnet and as a channel[15] (with two-way current), *draws* us Christ-ward. In another title, *Speculum Justitiae*, Mirror of Justice, she is regarded as a transparent reflection, *showing* Christ.

Cardinal Newman has reminded us that "the glories of Mary are for the sake of her Son." And St. Louis Marie de Montfort elaborates on this. "Let us not imagine...," he writes, "that Mary, being a creature, is a hindrance to our union with the Creator. It is no longer Mary who lives, it is only Jesus Christ, it is God alone Who lives in her.... Mary is the admirable echo of God. When we say 'Mary,' she answers, 'God.'"[16]

This saint was an outstanding champion of Our Lady's role. He is only one of many, many others. In fact, what saint was not an ardent lover of Mary? Could this be the reason they are saints? St. Louis Marie de Montfort has written a monumental work well named *True Devotion to Mary*. It is neither pietistic nor sentimental, but profoundly theological and conforms to St. Thomas's definition of devotion: "promptness of the will in the service of God."[17] It has received the accolade of all the recent popes, from Pius IX onward.

The saint draws upon countless references from the Fathers and Doctors of the Church who are unanimous, practically in identical wording, in declaring that Mary's role is to lead us to Christ. It is because of this foundation from Tradition that in Mariology (especially in its recent stepped-up studies and research) we discover the axiom: To Jesus through Mary.

Being visible, the relation between Mary and the Son is easy for us to perceive. But if seeing the "whole Christ" is to see Him in His place in the Trinity, the same is true for Mary. Everything—in fact, everything— starts and ends with the Trinity. Nothing can exist outside this focus. The telling of its secret must tell all secrets. Among all purely human and angelic natures it shines most brilliantly through this most glorious of creatures, Mary.

The inexhaustible scope of her motherhood is not completed until we see it in relation to the Father. Mary saw this and she wants us to see it too. Would she hold back secrets from her children? Did she not tell her cousin, Elizabeth, "He who is mighty has done great things for me" (Luke 1:49)?

We read of an added reason, relating to the Father, for the spotlessness of her "virginal-maternity" in the birth of the Son: "Not only is she a virgin, but her soul is stainless. The liturgy reveals to us that God's special design in granting to Mary the unique privilege of the Immaculate Conception was the prepare for His Word a dwelling place worthy of Him: 'O God, Who by the Immaculate Conception of the Virgin didst prepare a worthy dwelling-place for Thy Son' (Collect for the feast of the Immaculate Conception). Mary was to be the Mother of God; and this eminent dignity required not only that she should be a virgin, but that her purity should surpass that of the angels and be a reflection of the holy splendor wherein the Father begets His Son...The bosom of God, of infinite purity, is the dwelling place of the Only-begotten Son of God. The Word is ever *in the bosom of the Father*; but, in becoming Incarnate, He also willed, in ineffable condescension, to be *in the bosom of the Virgin Mother*. It was necessary that the tabernacle that Our Lady offered Him should recall, by its incomparable purity, the indefectible brightness of the light eternal where as God He ever dwells: 'Divinity was the bosom in God the Father, virginity in the Mother Mary'" (Sermon XII, Works of St. Ambrose).[18]

The Father "overshadowed" Mary (if invisibly, the more intimately) because of His daughter "she was the first of all creatures, the most acceptable child of God, the nearest and the dearest to Him" (Cardinal Newman). But also by her motherhood Mary "contracts a certain affinity with the Father" (Lepicier). In her "extended incarnations" she was to bear Him innumerable other Christs as brothers for His "Firstborn." "God the Father communicated to Mary His fruitfulness, inasmuch as a mere creature was capable of it, in order that He might give her power to produce His Son and all the members of His Mystical Body."[19] The "overshadowing" of Mary by the Father is not something historic, merely of the past. It continues till the end of time, as Christ continues to be born anew with every grace given to men—grace coming from the Father, by the Son, in the Holy Spirit, all *through* the motherliness of Mary. "Every grace that is communicated to this world comes by a threefold course, being dispensed in the most orderly fashion from God to Christ, from Christ to the Virgin, and from the Virgin to us."[20]

It was to St. Joseph, second to Mary in the hierarchy of excellence among creatures, that an angel of the Lord told *how* the Son of God became Incarnate: "Do not be afraid, Joseph, son of David, to take to thee Mary thy wife, for that which is begotten in her is of the Holy Spirit" (Matthew 1:20). This we echo in the Apostles Creed: "His only Son, our Lord, who was conceived by the Holy Spirit."

Here, by virtue of Mary's unique relation with the Trinity, we see in her another counterpart to the Divine Family. As her virginity was mystically related to the bosom of the Father, so it was related to the Holy Spirit Who made her fruitful by the Incarnation, whereby she became mystically His "spouse." The "work" of the Incarnation is attributed to the Holy Spirit because it was one of love, and He is the Person of Love. "God so *loved* the world that He sent His only-begotten Son." Mary willingly offered the sanctuary of her virginal womb; the Holy Spirit miraculously created the sacred humanity that filled it with the Son of God, when the "Word was made flesh."

Mary's union with her Divine Spouse is no less perpetual than that with the Father and the Son. We see this in the dramatic setting of Pentecost when she is centered in the midst of the apostles under the Cenacle's chandelier of flaming Tongues. St. Luke mentions her by name in detailing the prayerful preparations during the nine days prior to this tremendous event: "All these with one mind continued steadfastly in prayer with the women and Mary, the mother of Jesus" (Acts 1:14). On the Day of the Descent, "the scene and the actors are the same."[21]

It is obvious that chief among those praying was Mary. The promised Paraclete came, but He came through the praying mediatrix. It had to be so, for such was in the plan. The Son is the author of this first flood of graces to the Mystical Body. But the Holy Spirit is the fashioner of the members according to the pattern of the Incarnate Word. From that day on, He operates in faithful conjunction with His spouse, His "prime minister" of grace.

Familiarity with Mary inevitably leads to familiarity with the Divine Bond that unites us firmly to God's Love. "When the Holy Ghost, her Spouse, has found Mary in a soul, He flies there. He enters there in His fullness; He communicates Himself to that soul abundantly, and to the full extent to which it makes room for His Spouse. Nay, one of the reasons why the Holy Ghost does not now do startling wonders in our souls is because He does not find there a sufficiently great union with His faithful and inseparable Spouse. I say inseparable Spouse, because since that Substantial Love of the Father and the Son has espoused Mary, in order to produce Jesus Christ, the Head of the elect, and Jesus Christ in the elect, then He has never repudiated her, because she has always been fruitful and faithful."[22]

It is only Hopkins who can capture so much Mariology in his unique poetic vein, under the captivating title, "The Blessed Virgin Compared to the Air We Breathe":

> Wild air, world-mothering air,
> Nestling me everywhere,
> This needful, never spent,
> And nursing element;
> My more than meat and drink;
> My meal at every wink;
> This air, which, by life's law,
> My lung must draw and draw
> Now but to breathe its praise
> Minds me in many ways
> Of her who not only
> Gave God's infinity
> Dwindled to infancy
> Welcome in womb and breast,
> Birth, milk, and all the rest
> But mothers each new grace
> That does now reach our race—
>
> She, wild web, wondrous robe,
> Mantles the guilty globe,
> Since God has let dispense
> Her prayers His providence
>
> And men are meant to share
> Her life as life does air,
> If I have understood,

She holds high motherhood
Towards all our ghostly good
And plays in grace her part
About man's beating heart,
Laying, like air's fine flood,
The deathdance in his blood:
Yet no part but what will
Be Christ our Saviour still.
Though much the mystery how,
Not flesh but spirit now
And makes, O marvelous!
New Nazareths in us,
Where she shall yet conceive
Him, morning, noon, and eve;
New Bethlehems, and be born
There, evening, noon, and morn—
Bethlehem or Nazareth,
Men may draw like breath
More Christ and baffle death.[23]

## *Notes*

1. St. Bernard, *Homily 4 on the Incarnation.*
2. Shakespeare's *Julius Caesar.*
3. Dom Bernard Orchard, M.A., ed., *Catholic Commentary on Holy Scripture* (New York: Nelson, 1952).
4. *Ad diem illum laetissimum*, Feb. 2, 1904.
5. Pius XII, Address at Marian Celebration in Rome, Nov. 1, 1954.
6. Reprinted by special permission of Hawthorn Books from *Mary the Mother of God* by L. J. Suenens. © Hawthorn Books, 70 Fifth Avenue, New York 11, New York.
7. Response, 8th Lesson, Feast of the Seven Sorrows.

8.  Suenens, *op. cit.*, p. 10.
9.  *Ibid.*, pp. 63–64.
10. *Ibid.*, pp. 105–106.
11. Encyclical on the Mystical Body.
12. Suenens, *op. cit.*, p. 107.
13. *Summa*, II, Q. 38, Art. 1.
14. *Summa*, III, Q. 26, Art. 1.
15. "That grace should return to the giver by the same channel through which it came" (St. Bernard, *Sermon 3 on the Vigil of the Nativity*).
16. *The Secret of Mary* (Bay Shore, N.Y.: Montfort Publications), No. 21.
17. *Summa*, II, Q. 82, Art. 1.
18. Dom Columba Marmion, O.S.B., *Trinity in Our Spiritual Life* (Westminster, Md.: Newman Press, 1953), pp. 270–71.
19. St. Louis Marie de Montfort, *True Devotion to Mary* (Bay Shore, N.Y.: Montfort Publications), No. 17, p. 12.
20. St. Bernardine of Siena, *Sermon 6 on the Annunciation*.
21. Orchard, *op. cit.*, p. 1024.
22. De Montfort, *op. cit.*, No. 36, p. 23.
23. *Poems of Gerard Manley Hopkins* (London and New York: Oxford University Press, 1956), p. 99.

# Family Adoptions

At this stage we really reach "the heart of the matter." To the question "Why did the Son of God become man?" St. Augustine gives the answer, by shock treatment, if you will: "God became man that man might become God." Blasphemous? Not really. We have told about the Son as author of grace, the Holy Spirit as giver of grace, and Mary as the dispenser. Just what were we talking about? Something beautifully vague and intangible? By no means. Sanctifying grace is the most concrete of realities. In grace the soul becomes divine by participation in the nature of the Son of God, His Father, Their Love.

How does this come about? It may strike us as strange, but we are all "adopted children." When we call sanctifying grace "divine life" or the Christ-Life, we say what it means. When theologians speak of this grace, they really sum up that tidal-flood of Divine Life within the Godhead which is communicated to angels and to human souls. So also in regard to the "Family circle" we speak of "divine adoption" by the Father, making us brothers with His Firstborn, in fellowship with Their Spirit of Love.

If you know people who adopt babies, you know what a strenuous procedure they go through before the papers are finally signed. In becoming divinely adopted, we, too, go through a procedure, but by a much simpler process; simpler because divine. Divine methods are always less complicated than human ones. In contrast to the legal involvement of human adoption, there is the graciousness of ceremony in divine adoption. It is through baptism, as you well know, that "we become children of God." This initiates us into the sacramental system which, in the divine economy, furnishes the points of contact between divinity and humanity. Established by Christ Himself, the sacraments give us this sharing of Divine Life.

Received first in baptism, Divine Life grows and deepens with reception of the other sacraments, much the same as our human life is born, nourished, matured, fortified, and healed. Through prayer and the use of the utterly simple elements of water, oil, bread, and wine —outward signs of inward grace—the tremendous powers of the Christ-Life flow into our human lives and lift them up to the realm of divinity. This is the "life more abundant" to which Christ referred; this is the "gift of God" mentioned to the woman at the well. This brings us up to the supernatural, the superhuman plane, a third order of existence attained through the Incarnation. The first is the divine level, the second the human or natural, and the third is the supernatural, effected by the wedding of divinity with humanity.

Because all this starts with "adoption," we find adoption is stressed in Sacred Scripture and by the Fathers of the Church. Thus, St. John writes: "To as many as received him, he gave the *power* of becoming *sons of God*" (John 1:12). Hear St. Peter: "Who has called us by his own glory and power—through which he has granted us the very great and precious promises, so that through them you may becomes *partakers of the divine nature*" (2 Peter 1:3–4). And St. Paul: "Blessed be the God and Father of our Lord Jesus Christ, who has blessed us with every spiritual blessing on high in Christ.... He predestined us to be *adopted* through Jesus Christ as his *sons*, according to the purpose of his will, unto the praise of the glory of his grace, with which he has favored us in his beloved Son" (Ephesians 1:3, 5–6). And St. Paul again: "For those whom he has foreknown he has also predestined to become *conformed* to the *image* of his *Son*, that he should be the firstborn among many *brethren*" (Romans 8:29).

Listen to the echoes of Scripture in the voices of Tradition: "The gift surpassing all gifts is that God calls *man* His *child*, and that man calls God his Father."[1] "The Word became man for this reason, that man by accepting the Word and receiving the *grace* of *sonship* might become the *Son of God*."[2]

This adoption—our sonship through baptism —then, lifts us into the orbit of the supernatural where we gain an entry to the Divine Family. We are thereby taken into the circuit of the Trinitarian life through Christ, the Son, as the focal point of our entrance. We are now "at home." We can never really understand the supernatural until we see it as the "atmosphere" in which we now live "naturally" with the Trinity of Persons. In other words, the Trinity is the root of grace.

We must remember that in all exterior operations the Three work together as the inseparable Family. So it is the Trinity that adopts us into Their common life. But here, as in all our relations with God, it is most beneficial to see the distinct "appropriate" relations that divine adoption gives us with each Person. This is another reason for the telling of the secret; that we might have greater appreciation of the wonders given to us.

Thus the Father begets us as His adopted sons, as He eternally generates the Word. In baptism Christ is born again in us. By divine ingenuity we are reborn as "many brethren." His Father is our Father. In His tender farewell at His final departure from earth the Son said: "I ascend to my Father and your Father" (John 20:17).

Being "conformed to the image of his *Son*, that he should be the firstborn among many brethren," by adoption definitely makes the Son our brother. Time and time again Christ used the expression "My brethren"; and this not only in referring to the chosen twelve. Recall his touching words: "As long as you did it for one of these, the *least of my brethren*, you did it for me"

(Matthew 25:40). What clearer explanation of "brothers" than "other Christs"?

Adoption relates us to the Holy Spirit, as seen in St. Paul: "And because you are sons, God has sent the Spirit of his Son into our hearts" (Galatians 4:6). And, as the Liturgy has it in the Preface for Pentecost: "We give thanks to Thee, O holy Lord, *Father* Almighty, eternal God, *through Christ*, our Lord, Who ascending above all the heavens, and sitting at Thy right hand, did this day send down upon the children of *adoption* the *Holy Spirit* Whom He had promised." It is the Holy Spirit Who breathes forth, through love, the *divine life of grace* that *makes* us other Christs.

The Incarnate Son, in explaining the necessity of our adoption through baptism here below, as a requisite for eternal membership in the Divine Family, places the issue with simple brilliant clarity under the facet of rebirth. Speaking to Nicodemus, Jesus said: "'Amen, amen, I say to thee, unless a man be born again, he cannot see the kingdom of God.' Nicodemus said to him, 'How can a man be born when he is old? Can he enter a second time into his mother's womb and be born again?'" Jesus answered, 'Amen, amen, I say to thee, unless a man be born again of water and the Spirit, he cannot enter into the kingdom of God. That which is born of the flesh is flesh; and that which is born of the Spirit is spirit. Do not wonder that I said to thee, "You must be born again" (John 3:3–7). What could be more necessary than adoption?

The liturgy, which is Christ praying in His Mystical Body, sings of the experience of adoption magnificently and theologically in the glorious Easter Vigil ceremony:

> Almighty and everlasting God, be present at these mysteries of Thy great goodness, be present at these sacraments: and send forth the spirit of adoption to regenerate the new people, whom the font of baptism brings forth to Thee; that what is to be done by our humble ministry may be accomplished by the effect of Thy power. Through our Lord Jesus Christ, Thy Son, who liveth and reigneth with Thee in the unity of the Holy Spirit.... It is fitting indeed and just, right and helpful to salvation, for us always and everywhere to give thanks, O Holy Lord, Father Almighty, Everlasting God, Who by Thy invisible power dost wonderfully produce the effect of Thy sacraments. And though we are unworthy to perform such great mysteries, yet, as Thou dost not abandon the gifts of Thy grace, so Thou inclinest the ears of Thy goodness, even to our prayers. O God, Whose Spirit in the very beginning of the world moved over the waters, that even then the nature of water might receive the virtue of sanctification; O God Who by water didst wash away the crimes of the guilty world, and by the pouring out of the deluge didst give a figure of regeneration, that one and the same element might in a mystery be the end of vice and the beginning of virtue; look O Lord on the face of Thy

> Church, and multiply in her Thy regenera-
> tion, Who by the streams of Thy abundant
> grace fillest Thy city with joy, and dost open
> the font of Baptism for the renewal of the
> Gentiles throughout the world; that by the
> command of Thy Majesty she may receive the
> grace of Thy only-begotten Son from the Holy
> Spirit. May He by a secret mixture of His
> divine power, render this water fruitful for
> the regeneration of men, so that a heavenly
> offspring, conceived in sanctification, may
> emerge from the immaculate womb of this
> divine font, reborn a new creature; and grace
> as a mother may bring forth everyone, how-
> ever distinguished either by sex in body, by
> age in time, to the same infancy.

And the divine reason of this privileged favor of adoption? Again for the answer we look to St. John, the
authority on the love of God: "Behold what manner of
love the Father has bestowed upon us, that we should be
called children of God; and such we are" (1 John 3:1).

> When, in prayer, we consider this liberality
> and these advances towards us on the part of
> God, we feel the need for prostrating our-
> selves in adoration, and of singing a song of
> thanksgiving to the praise of the Infinite
> Being Who stoops towards us to give us the
> name of children. "Thou hast multiplied thy
> wonderful works, O Lord, my God, and there
> is no one like unto thee in thy plans for us"
> (Psalms 39:6).[3]

## *Notes*

1.    St. Leo, *Sermon 6 on the Nativity*.
2.    Irenaeus, *Adversus haereses*, Book III, C. 2.
3.    Dom Columba Marmion, *Christ the Life of the Soul* (St. Louis: Herder, 1922), p. 8.

# TWELVE

# Family Dwellings

Now we tell, not of the reason of the Incarnation, but of its flowering, its full bloom. For, indeed, in its fullness the secret lies nestling within our souls. This is the climax of all wonders. All that remains still hidden of the secret is the time and place when its radiance will shine forth visibly—as an open secret.

How does it come about that we are plunged in the heart of the Trinity by adoption? Is it that "papers are signed" for future living in this intimacy in heaven, God's home with its "many mansions"; and that, in the meantime, we are left as "orphans" in exile? By no means. Your heaven begins here. Life here is (or should be) heaven on earth.

You have heard of people having more than one home? Homes in New York and in Maine and in Florida, too? If (some) men can afford more than one, what about God? Yes, the inexhaustible riches of the Divine Family make it quite possible to have as many dwellings as there are angels and human beings. There is not a single "No Vacancy" sign shutting out this Family in the angelic world. There are many such signs in our world. "He came unto his own, and his own received him not. But to as many as *received* him he gave the power of becoming sons of God" (John 1:11–12).

Sanctifying grace, then, not only makes us adopted children of the Trinity, but when They adopt us They take up residence in our souls! With baptism we become Christ-bearers, temples of the Holy Spirit, dwellings of the Father, tabernacles of the Trinity! Dwelling within our souls, the Three Divine Persons live Their life therein; and *we*, because of such intimacy, join this Triune life. This is the meaning of what spiritual writers call "living (a conscious) interior life," and theologians call "the divine indwelling." Actually we are citizens of two worlds. We live two lives simultaneously: natural and supernatural, or better, human and divine. And what is the source of our knowledge of this seemingly incredible fact? Christ Himself.

The Incarnate Son of God saved His most sublime and tender words for His farewell message to His chosen friends. Again, by gesture of divine delicacy, the disciple "whom Jesus loved," and allowed to rest his head on the sacred bosom, is the sole recorder of these words of great import. It seems most probable that Christ spoke them immediately after the first Mass, offered at a supper table, and after the first "First Holy

Communion," unique also in that it was the first ordination of priests.

He created an atmosphere of the most intimate familiarity. On this occasion, He addressed His apostles as "little children"—again as "friends," not "servants" (only a friend conveys secrets to friends). He put them beautifully at their ease. Above all, this message was to be consoling. This was a calm prelude before His agony —and theirs. This was His touching souvenir for them, and for us. We must listen to Him through John whose words are almost entirely those of Our Savior:

> "Let not your heart be troubled. You believe in God; believe also in me.... I am the way, and the truth, and the *life*, No one comes to the Father but through me.... Dost thou not believe that I am *in* the Father and the Father *in* me? The words that I speak to you I speak not on my own authority. But the Father *dwelling* in me, it is he who does the works. Do you believe that I am in the Father and the Father in me?... If you love me, keep my commandments. And I will ask the Father and he will give you another Advocate to *dwell* with you forever, the *Spirit* of truth whom the world cannot receive, because it neither sees him nor knows him. But you shall know him, because he will *dwell* with you, and be *in* you.
>
> "I will not leave you orphans; I will come to you. Yet a little while and the world no longer sees me. But you see me, for I live and you shall *live*. In that day you will know that I am

>    *in* my Father, and *you in me*, and *I in you*. He
>    who has my commandments and keeps them,
>    he it is who loves me. But he who loves me
>    will be loved by my Father and I will love him
>    and *manifest* myself to him."
>
>    Judas, not the Iscariot, said to him: "Lord,
>    how is it that thou art about to *manifest* thy-
>    self to us, and not to the world?" Jesus
>    answered and said to him: "If anyone loves
>    me, he will keep my word, and my Father will
>    love him, and *we will come to him and make
>    our abode with him....*
>
>    "These things I have spoken to you while
>    yet dwelling with you. But the Advocate, the
>    *Holy Spirit*, whom the *Father* will send in *my*
>    name, he will teach you all things, and *bring
>    to your mind whatever I have said to you.*
>
>    "Peace I leave with you, *my peace I give to
>    you*; not as the world gives do I give to you. Do
>    not let our heart be troubled, or be *afraid*"
>    (John 14).

Here we have the secret, told many times before, retold
here, at the end, as on its highest note, in a finale that
rings with limpid clarity; the secret, as it were, "local-
ized" in the treasure-trove of the human soul.

With exquisite reserve St. John lets these sublime words rest on the authority of the Word, speaking.
We read his only commentary in the first of his three
brief Epistles. Some call this a "postscript" to his Gospel.
Here we find echoes of the final telling of the secret:

"And he who keeps his communication *abides* in
God, and God *in him*. And in this we know that he *abides*

in us, by the *Spirit* whom he has *given us*" (1 John 3:24). "In this has the love of God been shown in our case, that God has sent his only-begotten Son into the world that we may *live through him*" (1 John 4:9). "In this we know that *we abide in him and he in us*, because he has given us of his *Spirit*. And we have seen, and do testify that the *Father* has sent his *Son* to be the Savior of the world. Whoever confesses that Jesus is the Son of God, God *abides in him* and *he in God*" (1 John 4:13–15).

But there is no reserve in St. Paul. He, after John, is the authority on the divine indwelling. Could it be that when, on his way to Damascus to persecute the Christians, a blinding light felled him to the ground and he heard the divine voice that converted him, this so set his heart on fire that he is known as the "burning Apostle"? His phrases fly out like sparks from the Epistles; letters written, not to scholars or theologians, but to his dearly beloved, recent converts. No one can write like this unless he *lives* to the full the life of grace. He uses the word "grace" one hundred times, and we find neatly "packaged" in his Epistles the impact of divine adoption and indwelling:

"It is now no longer I that live, but Christ lives in me. And the life that I now live in the flesh, I live in the faith of the Son of God...I do not cast away the grace of God" (Galatians 2:20–21). "Your life is hidden with Christ in God" (Colossians 3:3). "For you are all the children of God through faith in Christ Jesus. For all you who have been baptized into Christ, have put on Christ." (Galatians 3:26–27). "For me to live is Christ and to die is gain" (Philippians 1:21). "For as the body is one and has many members, and all the members of the body, many as they are, form one body, so also it is with Christ. For in one Spirit were all baptized into one body" (1 Corinthians 12:12–13). "Or do you not know that your members are the temple of the Holy Spirit, who is in you, whom you have from God, and that you are not your own?" (1 Corinthians 6:19). "For you are the temple of the living God" (2 Corinthians 6:16). "For whoever are led by the Spirit of God, they are the sons of God. Now you have not received a spirit of bondage so as to be again in fear, but you have received a spirit of adoption as sons, by virtue of which we cry, 'Abba! Father!' The Spirit himself gives testimony to our spirit that we are sons of God" (Romans 8:14–16).

Grace a complicated subject? Christ did not complicate it at the supper table. Neither did John or Paul. John reservedly let it shine through the Light of the World. Paul turned the floodlights on it from every angle. St. Thomas did not complicate it. His treatment is crystal-clear, as he draws from John and Paul and from the Fathers of the Church.

True, it is mysterious and supernatural. Yet every three-week old infant, fresh from the bath of baptism, receives a *Gift* to understand (soon) the wonders within him. Yes, every baptized child is "gifted."

What are these wonders coursing through every baptized soul? Sanctifying grace is a prolongation of the Trinitarian processions; the Son proceeding from the Father, the Holy Spirit proceeding from the other Two, the while the soul is caught up into this divine vortex. The Father, while dwelling in the temple-soul, keeps sending His Son to us, and both breathe forth Their Love.

It is amazing, but very true, that the Father, dwelling within us, loves us with the *same* love that He eternally bestows on His Son. What other kind of love has He? More amazing still, we must love the Trinity with this same love. After being "deified" by adoption, what other kind of love have we that is worthy of God? Our natural love (and life) has been divinized. "God became man, that man might become God." *Noblesse oblige!* Loving with His love (supernaturally, in the state of grace, of course) takes only a flick of the will, an intention. For example, washing dishes, digging ditches, doing homework, suffering toothache—for (and with) the love of God. "Therefore, whether you eat or drink, or do anything else, do all for the glory of God" (1 Corinthians 10:31).

St. Thomas brings to light a most consoling facet of this magnificent divine indwelling through grace. The Father abides in us, together with His Son of Love, that we might *enjoy* Their presence in our soul.[1] Do you not see from this how intimate is our *sharing* as divine joy mingles with divinized joy? There is no getting away from the fact that nothing is as thrilling as the love of God!

Of course we have to work at it; that is, we have to cooperate (work together). Love is never a one-way proposition. Love is diffusive but always seeks a return. Divine love is no exception. But God makes it easy. He has been called the "Hound of Heaven," and hounds never give up.

He has made it easy by bestowing on us His very Life. He said, "I am the way, and the truth, and the life," and "I am come that they may have *life* and life *more abundant.*" What life? His Life, Divine Life, life of grace. Life, if it is to survive, must grow. The growth potential in Divine Life is unlimited. The more we use of this Life, the more we receive. There is no point of no return with grace. Once received, if exercised and developed, it yields "gifts" and "fruits" of abundance. This really means that with each increase the Divine Family only becomes more fully and deeply rooted in our soul. The Father's Image is brighter, His Gift is more "enjoyable." We feed this growth by prayer, the sacraments, and charity (good works).

There is a practical side to this "cooperating." If the beginning of our heaven starts here with the grace of adoption and divine indwelling, it becomes intimately related to the completion of our heaven. That is to say, the higher premiums we pay here, by efforts to develop our Divine Life, the bigger dividends we receive later. The magnificence of our "mansion" will be measured accordingly, not in bulk but in depth, the depth of our vision. The deepening process takes place here. We are, of course, talking about the vision of a Family.

St. Paul, always practical, reminds us that effort is imperative. The beauty of the "temples" that we are shines from within. It does not change the outer material—clay. "We carry this treasure in vessels of clay" (2 Corinthians 4:7). In other words, if "keeping His commandments" (together with baptism) brings the Trinity into our souls, breaking the commandments (seriously) dismisses Them. They return (ordinarily) only with the sacramental reception of grace—and time can run out.

We are living in a stepped-up age. Old methods have died, new methods are born each day. The stage-coaches, the horse and buggy, the sailing vessel are things of the past. District schools have replaced the little red schoolhouse. And of course we have *visual* education, all the way round. The phrase, "It's a small world," really dates you now. What with outer space it is getting rather big again. It has growing pains.

All this is to the good—if not overdone. By this I mean that all the modern visual education leads us nowhere if it interferes with the appreciation of, or education in, the *non-visual* wonders of the Trinity making Its abode in the souls of men. What are the Seven Wonders of the World compared to this—any seven you name? And what is the wonder of outer space compared with that of the soul—the pinnacle of the created world, where Creator abides with creatures? It is the *raison d'être* of everything created, visible or invisible, inner or outer. In fact, all visible wonders, past, present, and even future, are but settings and avenues for these pinnacles where God walks and lives with man.

The greatest danger stemming from the artificiality of mass communications is that people come to believe that anything lying outside the scope of these media is not worth communicating. And since the soul cannot be photographed, it must be quite negligible, quite expendable. Such philosophy ignores the words uttered by One who died to save souls. His death was their "great price," He said: "What does it profit a man, if he gain the *whole world*, but suffer the loss of his own soul?" (Matthew 16:26). A lost soul is nothing but a desecrated and empty temple.

Mass media has a kinship with mass hysteria. Both have a wide spread. Both form a false mentality; both are warped. What we are driving at is this: Overemphasis on the visible is dangerous. Without extra effort it is easy, even for those with spiritual vision, to succumb to this and neglect the "*evidence* of things that are *not seen*" (St. Paul's definition of faith, in Hebrews 11:1). Faith is one of the powers inherited with adoption. It is the key that unlocks the door to the treasure. It is a lens that gives vision beyond a silver screen, that puts the visible and the invisible in proper focus.

What a tragedy to neglect wonders within, for soap-bubble chasing! True, at the moment, soap opera glamour covers quite a range, but fortunately there are many brighter new horizons now visible. One of these is a vital interest in theology on the part of the laity. Adult study clubs have been formed; there are extension courses in theology. The Church goes in for "stepping-up" methods, too. She always keeps up with the times, with discretion of course. Religious instruction is widely given through Catholic information centers and bureaus and religious correspondence courses, as well as by means of radio and television, and there are excellent books on religion geared for the laity.

But speaking of horizons, the wider they are the more excitement there is in approaching them. It would be a shame, then, if in this new approach people should be "afraid" of the subject of the divine indwelling. Always, the thrill in seeking horizons is the challenge they offer. Explorers are never timid. After the first step, one has more assurance.

The point is, if the study of theology is fundamental (and it is) why give up before tasting the reward? The reward dwells within. Our chief concern, of course, is not study. This is only the approach leading to the reward. The Gospel (Trinity in detail) is not only to be studied, but primarily to be lived. The way and truth lead to life.

The precise aim of the new approach, through organized study and individual reading, is to develop the habit of *living* this life. Among the outstanding writings in this direction are the books of Raoul Plus, S.J. (*God within Us; Living with God,* etc.), Paul De Jaegher, S.J. (*The Lord Is My Joy*), M.V. Bernadot, O.P. (*From Holy Communion to the Blessed Trinity*)—to mention just a few. Written simply and with the utmost brevity, they speak to the average reader about the wonders of the indwelling and make it positively enticing. But, best of all, they introduce you to the greatest (popular) master of this subject in recent times, Sister Elizabeth of the Trinity, a Carmelite nun, born in France in 1880, whose name very recently was entered for beatification. The reason these writers quote her is because she made it all seem so natural and easy.

Her contemporary, St. Thérèse of Lisieux, is still showing us her Little Way to heaven, and Sister

Elizabeth is still showing us the Little Way to heaven-on-earth—"still showing," because since her death well over 100,000 copies (not counting a dozen translations into foreign languages) of Sister Elizabeth's *Souvenirs* have tumbled off the press. A recent translation into English, published for American readers, bears the title *The Spiritual Doctrine of Sister Elizabeth of the Trinity*,[2] edited by Marie-Michel Philipon, O.P. Father Philipon stresses the fact that Sister Elizabeth's familiarity with the divine indwelling rests on the strongest theological foundations. The great Cardinal Mercier kept the copy of the *Souvenirs* by his bedside and expressed the wish that all his priests would own this book.

A passage from the Preface sums up her message: "The servant of God, Elizabeth of the Trinity, was one of those enlightened souls and heroic souls able to cling to one of these great truths, which are both the *simplest* and the *most important*, and, beneath the appearance of an *ordinary life*, to find therein the secret of a very close union with God. This mystery of the indwelling of the Blessed Trinity in the depths of her soul was the great *reality* of her interior life. As she herself said: 'The Trinity! There is our dwelling, our home, the Father's house that we must never leave...It seems to me that I have found my heaven on earth, for heaven is God and God is in my soul.'"

Obviously, this soul, charming in her simplicity, did not write for publication. Her private journal came to light after her death. However, while she lived, she did not keep her secret to herself. In her visits to the convent parlor with her mother, relatives, friends, in fact with all who came in contact with her personally, as well as in all her many letters, she unobtrusively but persistently carried out her apostolate of the Divine Presence within the soul, "so that in every hour of the day and night, in every joy and sorrow, you may find Him there, quite near, within you."

This apostolate she promised to continue in her "visible" heaven, behind the scenes, with no thought on her part of any relation to her private *Souvenirs*. The "Trinity Whom she adored" had other plans. Shortly before her death, weakened by intense suffering, she said: "Believe that above, in the home of love, I shall take an active interest in you. I shall ask for a grace of union, of intimacy with the Master; that is what has made my life an anticipated heaven. It seems to me that in heaven my mission will be to draw souls, by helping them to go out of themselves in order to adhere to God by a very simple, wholly loving movement and to maintain them in that great inner silence which allows God to imprint Himself on them and to transform them into Himself." By the intervention of Divine Providence, the phenomenal circulation of the *Souvenirs* became contacts that furthered this promised apostolate.

Her promise "to take an active interest" in asking "for a grace of union" beautifully echoes that of her saintly sister from Lisieux, "I will spend my heaven in doing good upon earth." The one showers roses, the other souvenirs.

Commenting on the phrase "by helping them to go out of themselves," Philipon has this to say: "This is the grace of graces. How many souls never succeed in getting out of the thousand labyrinthine ways of self! The most fervent sigh over it and despair of so doing. In vain do they endeavor to free themselves by their own efforts which avail nothing. This is beyond men's strength and calls for the grace of God. Hence it is a very precious grace which the servant of God promises to all those interior souls imprisoned in their own egoism. From heaven, her silent intervention leads them to that complete liberation which casts them wholly upon Christ."[3]

It could well be that the prayers and present process for her canonization are timely, as a means to convert an age centered in self to one centered in Christ—and thence to one centered in the Trinity.

There is striking evidence that Sister Elizabeth's appeal is not solely to theologians, priests, and religious, in the following extract from a letter written, after the first appearance of the *Souvenirs*, by a humble, simple person in the world (typical of many other letters): "I did not know that the good God loved us so much, and that He was so close to us. No one had taught that as this little nun; and yet it is what preachers ought to teach. What we most need to know amid the troubles of this life is that the good God loves us, and that He is with us, in us."[4]

If this seems too "pious," how about the following? A military chaplain (World War I) sent this precious testimony from the Belgian front: "When anyone manages to make a serious-minded young man read the *Reminiscences*, he finds therein a pleasure, a strengthening, a life hitherto unsuspected. I have learned this by experience. These soldiers are wonderful in their interior life after such reading." And another: "The faith in the divine indwelling which Sister Elizabeth has revealed to them is a strong support when, with shrapnel and fire raining down upon them, they are deprived of the help of their chaplain."[5]

Some might be afraid that devotion to the Trinity would cause a cleavage between them and the historic and Eucharistic Christ, but nothing could be further from the truth. Every rosary "links" together the joyful, sorrowful, and glorious mysteries of Christ. Every Mass is Christmas, Good Friday, Easter, Ascension, Pentecost. Where you have the "whole" Christ, you find Him "linked" to the Father and the Holy Spirit. So it is that every adopted child, through baptism, is born, buried, risen, elevated in Christ, in union with the Father and the Holy Spirit. The most perfect way to meditate on the historic mysteries of Christ is to let Him relive them in us as we unite our joys, sorrows, triumphs with Him—in union with the Father and the Holy Spirit.

The Eucharist is a tangible gateway to the Trinity. A sacramental extension of the Incarnation, it reminds us from where and why the Son "appeared"; from the Father, as the "way" to the Father. Christ is really present in the Eucharist and He is simultaneously present in the bosom of the Father. To stop at the sacred humanity, in contemplation, is to miss the point of the

Blessed Sacrament. "God became man that man might become God." The Eucharistic Bread gives tremendous strength that deepens the divine indwelling within us. Christ unites us in the closet communion with Himself, through His Spirit of Love, to unite us to turn to the Father.[6]

Because Sister Elizabeth of the Trinity believed the message of the Last Supper, "We will come and make our abode with him," she was constantly aware of the Life within her. She remembered the words, "Let not your heart be troubled," and she was not afraid. No child is afraid in the protective embrace of his family. Sister Elizabeth shows us how to *live* in the embrace of the Divine Family, how to make that Divine Life within us *grow*, how to *enjoy* the company of our Father, Brother, Friend ("Sweet Guest of the soul," as we sing in the "Come, Holy Ghost").

We find her doctrine in the practical application through her celebrated prayer, "Trinity Whom I Adore,"[7] as well as in her multitudinous letters. She wrote no textbook. She drank in the doctrine from Christ's words at the Last Supper and from St. Paul's elaboration on them. She put the latter in the vernacular of our times, and like him lived what she professed. St. Paul should be enough, but, alas, it seems our age must have audio-visual education. If so, Sister Elizabeth is St. Paul via that medium.

Far from divorcing herself from personal devotion to Christ, Sister Elizabeth becomes Trinity-centered by first becoming more deeply Christ-centered. Christ is the center of the Trinitarian life in the Divine Family and in the soul.

In her prayer, after the words, "O my God, Trinity Whom I adore! Help me to become utterly forgetful of self, that I may bury myself in Thee," etc., she addresses each Person individually, starting with Christ:

> O my Christ, Whom I love...yet I realize my weakness and beseech Thee to clothe me with Thyself, to identify my soul with all the movements of Thine Own. Immerse me in Thyself; posses me wholly; substitute Thyself for me that my life may be a radiance of Thine own. Enter my soul as Adorer, as Restorer, as Savior!
>
> O Eternal Word, Utterance of my God! I long to pass my life in listening to Thee, to become docile that I may learn from Thee. Through all darkness, all privations, all helplessness, I crave to keep Thee ever with me and to dwell beneath Thy lustrous beams.

In calling on the other Two, see how she accents the "Center":

> O Consuming Fire! Spirit of Love! Descend within me and reproduce in me, as it were, an *incarnation* of the Word; that I may be to Him another *humanity* wherein He *renews* His *Mystery*!
>
> And Thou, O Father, bend down toward Thy poor little creature and overshadow her, *beholding* in her none other than *Thy Beloved Son* in whom Thou hast set all Thy pleasure.

This prayer, "one of the most beautiful in Christian literature" (Philipon), then closes: "O my 'Three,' my All, my Beatitude, Infinite Solitude, Immensity wherein I lose myself! Bury Thyself in me that I may be buried in Thee, until I depart to contemplate in Thy Light the abyss of Thy greatness!" Eminently practical, she misses nothing. Her public was extensive and cosmopolitan, embracing every class of readers, as the following excerpts from her correspondence show.

> Your weaknesses, your sins, all that is troubling you, is what He wishes to deliver you from by His continual contact. Has he not said that He comes not to judge but to save? Nothing hinders you from going to Him...Do not say that that is not for you, that you are too wretched; on the contrary, that is the reason the more for going to Him Who saves. It is not in looking at our miseries that we shall be cleansed, but by gazing upon Him Who is all purity and sanctity.[8]

Her consoling message is suited for every Christian who must wear the badge of Christ—the cross. Beautifully she lifts all human suffering to the plane of the divine:

> Rejoice in the thought that from all eternity we have been known of the Father, as St. Paul says, and that He wishes to find in us the image of His crucified Son. If you knew how necessary suffering is in order that God's work may be done in the soul! The good God had an immense desire to enrich us with His graces, but it is we who determine the amount

in proportion as we allow ourselves to be immolated by Him—immolated, like the Master, in joy, in thanksgiving, saying with Him: "The chalice which my Father hath given, shall I not drink it?" He called the hour of His Passion "His hour," that for which He had come, that for which He yearned with all His strength. When a great suffering, or a very small sacrifice is offered us, let us think quickly, that it is "our hour," the hour to prove our love for Him Who, as St. Paul says, loved us exceedingly.[9]

Three months before she departed for the "blessed Vision of peace," she wrote to her mother: "I wish I could tell all souls what a source of strength, peace, and happiness they would find by living in this intimate union of the Three Divine Persons."[10]

## *Notes:*

1. *Summa*, II, Q. 43, Art. 3, 4, 5.
2. Published by Newman Press (Westminster, Md.) in 1947, with Preface by Father Garrigou-Lagrange, O.P., and continued through recent printings.
3. Philipon, *op. cit.*, p. 207.
4. *Reminiscences (Souvenirs) of Sister Elizabeth of the Trinity*, edited by a Discalced Carmelite of Dijon (Westminster, Md.: Newman Press, 1952), p. 175.
5. *Ibid.*, pp. 180–181.
6. We refer the reader to M. V. Bernadot's *From the Holy Communion to the Blessed Trinity*.
7. The reader is referred to "Trinity Whom I Adore," a commentary (in *Meditations*) on this prayer, by Dom Eugene Vandeur, O.S.B. (Pustet, New York, 1953), in prayer-book format.

8.      Philipon, *op. cit.*, p. 75.
9.      Philipon, *op. cit.*, p. 120.
10.     Philipon, *op. cit.*, p. 104.

# THIRTEEN

# Family Prayer

What practical application follows from the doctrine of the divine indwelling besides the necessity of giving the Divine Family the courtesy of recognizing Their gracious presence and of speaking to Them intimately? We speak to Them publicly. This we call public prayer. Another name for prayer is conversation with God; expressed in the language of the soul. Prayer, of course, is the highest activity of the mind, heart, and soul. Human and angelic spirits achieve their fulfillment by "knowing" and "loving" the Divine Spirit through prayer.

To this we must add love for neighbor, which is proof of love for God. Prayer and charity are two sides of a single coin; one expresses love, the other means it. Prayerful conversation with God and works of charity are the greatest sources of developing the share of the Christ-Life we received in baptism. For our spiritual growth we need not only the increased strength we receive from the sacraments. We also need to perform works of charity and to pray. These are the means of increasing the grace received. We need spiritual exercise for the soul, just as we need physical exercise for the body, and this is provided by prayer and good works, which in turn dispose us for greater grace when we receive the sacraments.

We have to externalize, so to speak, our interior prayer life. We must express it outwardly. We have to lend "other humanities" to Christ that He might extend His Incarnation by building up a more vital Mystical Body to further His Father's business—but first of all we must pray. Remember the climax of His "business," finished (visibly) with the crucifixion, when being "lifted up" He drew all things to Himself. In so drawing all things (ourselves included) He lifted us with Himself to the Father in the greatest form of prayer, a sacrifice, expressing adoration, thanksgiving, reparation, and petition. It was the Blood of this sacrifice that purchased all those divine dwellings.

Christ's parting gift at His farewell supper was His abiding presence in the Eucharist which would be a perpetual reminder of the price He paid for these living temples. This same Eucharist is a sacrifice and a sacrament. As a sacrifice Christ reenacts His role of Victim on the Cross as the glorified Victim at the Mass; as a sacrament He gives us His resurrected Victim-Flesh to eat.

The Mass is identical with Calvary: the same Victim, the same sacrifice, the same mighty "Offertory

Prayer"; but there is one distinction, the bleeding wounds are now radiant with glory.

Why continue the offering that was more than adequate to redeem a million worlds? The Father does not need reminding. No, but we do. It is easy to forget. And to remind us the more, Christ sees to it that we all offer Him now. And even more, He insists that we offer our miserable selves at the same time He re-offers us to the Father. It is certainly not His fault if we forget.

Now we see the reason for public prayer, which we call the liturgy, a word that is more technical than descriptive. For what is the liturgy if not Christ prayer in His Mystical Body, the Son of God made flesh now manifesting Himself in a sacramental, visible ensemble of human words, actions, and processions, in a dramatic yet harmonious setting of music, lights, bells, incense, furnishings (tables both sacrificial and banquet, fonts, steps, benches, hangings, carpets, gold, silver, marble, wood), water, bread, wine, oil, palm branches, and blessed ashes? In short, divinity shining, speaking, singing, fragrant, through things that reach our senses and break through to our souls, the while these carry us out of ourselves and unite us with the Mystic Christ, "lifted up," drawing all things to Himself in the company of the Family; joining in counterpoint the angelic choirs celebrating the liturgy with their incessant *Sanctus, Sanctus, Sanctus*, as we hymn *Gloria Patri, et Filio et Spiritui Sancto*. This is the liturgy.

From this description we see that it is a mistake to associate with the liturgy only the Mass. While this magnificent spectacle and drama is the heart and soul of the liturgy, there are arteries that flow from it, bringing us the divine life-stream of grace, the sap uniting the vine and the branches (John 5:15); uniting us as "members of his body" (Ephesians 5:30).

The most vital of these extensions of the Mass are the other six sacraments of which the Eucharist is the source and the goal. So, St. Thomas reminds us: "The sacrament of holy orders is obviously ordained to the consecration of the Eucharist. The sacrament of baptism is ordained to the reception of the Eucharist. Such also is the orientation of Confirmation. Again, through penance and extreme unction man is prepared to receive the Body of Christ worthily. Matrimony also is referred to this sacrament, at least by its symbolism, insofar as it represents the union of Christ and the Church, of which the sacrament of the Eucharist is a figure."[1]

And we cannot exclude from the scope of the liturgy those seventy-times-seven "grace-full" fringes called sacramentals, little sacraments, far less powerful, yet significant and purposeful. We dare not despise them, for we can never look down upon but must look up at carriers of grace. "The Spirit breathes where he will": now in the roaring of the wind, now in the gentle whisper of a breeze. Do you realize that there are more than two hundred sacramental blessings in the official Ritual of the Church for things in sacred and profane daily use, ranging from bells to bees? It was robust, not superstitious, faith that prompted the sick to entreat Christ "to let them touch but the tassel of his cloak; and all who touched it were saved" (Matthew 14:36).

Some might frown upon the sacraments because they were "only" instituted by the Church. But who is the Church, if not Christ? One of the loveliest sacramentals is the Mandatum on Holy Thursday. It first took place at the Last Supper when the Master commanded twelve fishermen that they allow Him to wash their feet.

Another way to see the liturgy is to see it as a cluster of living temples, praying, lifting the Son to the Father, being caught up in this mutual offering of the Divine Victim joined to living temples; extended, externalized Christs, who receive back from the Father, externally, the Victim as nourishment and embellishment of the temple of their individual souls. This public praying together is necessary because God is the Creator of society as well as of individuals. This public praying together is not necessary because God is the Creator of the society as well as of individuals. Society is another name for the vast extension of the Divine Family. We must belong to, and take part in, the entire Family life. In this Family, just as in a human family, each member takes his part in family living, while at the same time not losing, but rather developing, his own personality and personal contribution. Each family unit is an intimate grouping of individuals—father differing distinctly from mother; each child individual and distinct from every other child.

In the foregoing explanation of the liturgy, we have tried to anticipate a possible question. For those to whom the teaching of the divine indwelling may be something new (it is actually as old as the Last Supper), there may appear to be a conflict in reconciling this with the recent liturgical movement (also as old as the Last Supper). The domain of one is interior, of the other exterior. At first sight this seems like a duplication that would weaken each. And of course external action is so much easier to appreciate and negotiate. But right here we see the greatest danger and drawback which can result from a mistaken notion of "active participation" in the Mass. To see and enter into the external action of the Mass is not to see the Mass at all. The Mass is not merely a spectacle nor a concerted exercise of vocal and physical activity. Stirring people from lethargy to external participation is only the first step; the second step leads to interior participation.

Pope Pius XII makes this point very plain:

> The worship rendered by the Church to God must be, in its entirety, interior as well as exterior. It is exterior because the nature of man as a composite being requires it to be so. Likewise, because Divine Providence has disposed that 'while we recognize God visibly, we may be drawn by Him to love of things unseen' (Roman Missal).... But the chief element of divine worship must be interior. For we must always live in Christ and give ourselves to Him completely, so that in Him, with Him, and through Him the heavenly Father may be duly glorified. The sacred Liturgy requires, however, that both these elements be intimately linked with each

> other...Otherwise religion clearly amounts to
> mere formalism, without meaning and with-
> out content.[2]

In other words, active participation is not merely togetherness, beautifully going through the motions of worship.
We have to alert our minds and hearts to what each word
and action means and enter into communication in the
idiom of sacramental signs (words, actions, things).

This interior quality of the offering of Christ and
ourselves in the Mass becomes related to our interior
divine dwelling in the downward movement of the
Mass—the Communion, starting with Our Father, when
we receive back the Divine Victim from the Father, as we
partake in the sacred banquet, eating the sacrificial
Lamb to nourish the Divine (Triune) Life within our
souls, as already mentioned. Communication of graces,
stemming from the Cross (and hence from the Mass),
continues through the other sacraments and sacramentals of the liturgy. You see, again, the absence of conflict,
resolved in the union of the external liturgical action
with interior deepening of the divine indwelling.

It becomes furthermore necessary to highlight
this reconciliation, because in some quarters overzealous
enthusiasts for the liturgy have openly declared opposi-
tion between the two. Another name for developing in
depth the divine indwelling is contemplation—thinking
about the Divine Presence within, talking (praying)
to the Three Who abide there (at least this is the greatest reality we can mediate on or contemplate; the goal
of every baptized Christian is thus to begin heaven

on earth). Using this term (contemplation, meditation, or any other form of interior personal praying), some superficial thinking on the liturgy condemns all this, preferring what they term "objective piety" only; which, in the light of what we have seen, is much ado about nothing.

Again, in no uncertain words the learned Pontiff condemns this false attitude:

In this connection, We desire to direct your attention to certain recent theories touching a so-called "objective" piety. While these theories attempt, it is true, to throw light on the mystery of the Mystical Body, on the effective reality of sanctifying grace,...it is nonetheless apparent that they tend to belittle, or pass over in silence, what they call "subjective" or "personal" piety.... As a result they feel that all other religious exercises not directly connected with the sacred Liturgy and performed outside public worship should be omitted. But though the principles set forth above are excellent, it must be plain to everyone that the conclusions drawn from them respecting the two sorts of piety are false, insidious, and quite pernicious.[3]

The encyclical explains the necessity of personal piety. In the very beginning of the letter, Pope Pius cites first the obligation of the individual to honor God: "This duty is incumbent, first of all, on men as individuals. But it also binds the whole community of human beings...."[4]

After all, to see conflict now in these two subjects is to put conflict in the context of Christ's discourse at the Last Supper. It was the same Teacher Who promised "We will come to him and make our abode with him" (this, in all probability *after* the "First Mass") and Who promised to abide with us in the sacrifice-sacrament of the Eucharist. No one has ever accused this Teacher of confusing an issue. Never did He teach clearer than by example. How many years for His public, external mission? Three. How many for His "hidden" life of contemplation? Thirty. (The way to follow Christ is to follow Him all the way.)

The Mystical Body at prayer is a Divine Family at prayer, as we have seen. What is not so easy is to see the presence of the Divine Family, without Whom there just would be no prayer at all. True, the members sense the presence of their Head (we hope); the branches should know their union with the vine. But always it is an inseparable Family. This apparent unawareness of the association of the Father and the Holy Spirit reflects the lack of alertness to the very wording of the Mass.

Do you realize that we do not address Christ, personally and alone, until we come to the Agnes Dei? And that up to this point, from the Offertory, through the Canon, into the Communion, we call on the Father, personally, at least twenty times, not to mention the several pronouns referring to Him? Surely such awareness should help us realize more keenly that the Mass is essentially an offering and a receiving of Christ, to and from the Father. These very words, "Father," "Son," "accept," "give," show us the purposeful structure of the Mass: its upward and downward movement.

Nor is the Holy Spirit, as a Person distinct from Father and Son, left unmentioned in the Mass. It is useful to recall that the final prayer of the Offertory is addressed to Him alone: "Come, Thou Sanctifier, Almighty and Eternal God, and bless this sacrifice prepared for the glory of Thy holy Name."

When we come to calling on the Three Divine Persons together, it may be from its very frequency that we are scarcely conscious of this privilege. Surely such a privileged intimacy should arouse us from the area of the unconscious. The tremendous vista into the Divine that is the Mass opens in the name of the Father and of the Son and of the Holy Spirit. The Kyrie is an abridged litany, dramatic with three, terse repetitious invocations to each Person, begging for mercy so that we may become more worthy to do what we are doing. In a switch from the minor key, we follow immediately with an expansive hymn of praise and love, singing the *Glory* of the Father, Son, and Holy Spirit.

Interesting variety that helps to make us more alert comes into the Mass each day through nine prayers that are different from, and inserted between, the ones that never change. Among these is the Collect, or chief prayer of the day. Here we almost always invoke the Father, making some special petition, but always concluding our request: "Through our Lord Jesus Christ, Thy Son, who liveth and reigneth with Thee in the unity of the Holy Spirit, God, world without end" (sometimes with varied wording). We see the same pattern in each Secret and Postcommunion prayer.

In the Credo we engage in a magnificent chorus, a prolonged Amen and profession of faith in the Trinity, praying all the theology of the mysteries of creation, incarnation, redemption, sanctification, effected by the Three Divine Persons.

In the Preface, especially that of the Trinity, said nearly every Sunday and weekday, we set to prayer even more precise theology of the Trinity, accenting the "distinction in persons, oneness in being and equality in majesty," Then we join the chorus of angels in a triple outburst of *Sanctus, Sanctus, Sanctus,* mingled with Hosannas. When sung, the melody of the Preface and Sanctus is incomparable to any heard on earth.

After calling on Christ three times, in familiarity, as the Lamb of God, we address three intimate prayers to Him, begging for the peace which He promised to leave us and for more worthiness to partake of His Flesh, as the Bread of our life. In the central prayer of this group we acknowledge the presence of His Father and the Holy Spirit: "O Lord Jesus Christ, Son of the living God, Who, by the will of the Father and the cooperation of the Holy Spirit, hast by Thy death given life to the world: deliver me by this Thy most sacred Body and Blood from all my sins and from all evil...Who with the same God the Father and the Holy Spirit, livest and reignest, God, world without end. Amen."

The last prayer of the Mass is the beautiful *Placeat*: "May the tribute of my worship be pleasing to Thee, most holy Trinity, and grant that the sacrifice which I, all unworthy, have offered in the presence of Thy

Majesty, may be acceptable to Thee, and may, through Thy mercy, obtain forgiveness for me and all for whom I have offered it. Through Christ our Lord. Amen."

The Mass ends as it began: "May God almighty bless you: the Father, the Son, and the Holy Spirit. Amen."

As St. Thomas has told us, all the other sacraments relate to the Eucharist, Mass and Sacrament. In the miracle of the Mass, time and space disappear, as Calvary, with its price of blood, becomes present. The Eucharistic Sacrament contains not only increased measures of the Christ-Life, but the living Christ in Person. For this reason the Church bids us "compare the Eucharist to the fountain, the other sacraments to rivulets. For the Holy Eucharist is truly and necessarily to be called the fountain of all graces, containing as it does, after an admirable manner, the fountain itself of celestial gifts and graces, and the Author of all the sacraments, Christ our Lord, from whom, as from its source, is derived whatever of goodness and perfection the other sacraments possess."[5] Because of this intimate relation between the Mass and the sacraments we find the Trinity permeating the entire liturgy.

Baptism, as we know, adopts us as members of the Divine Family, Who immediately take up residence in our souls, as practically the first prayer reminds us in the magnificent ceremonies of the administration of this sacrament: "Receive the sign of the Cross on your forehead and in your heart. Have faith in the teachings of

God, and live in such a way that from now on you may be enabled to be a temple of God."

As these significant ceremonies unfold, the priest commands Satan to depart and "give place to the Holy Spirit, the Consoler." He addresses the Father, personally, six times; the Son, eight; and the Three together, six. Besides this, there is the recitation of the Creed and a profession of faith in each Divine Person. Initiation finally takes place "in the name of the Father, and of the Son, and of the Holy Spirit."

Baptism makes us adopted children of God. But as the Divine Child "grew in age and wisdom" (humanly), so His adopted brothers must grow with His Divine Life into maturity. Confirmation is the sacrament that provides for this. The very word means to make intensely firm. With confirmation the Christ-Life attains firmness in depth. This sacrament brings the Christ-Life to complete maturity, as it strengthens the supernatural powers received in baptism: faith, hope, charity. There should be nothing strange in the fact that in the early Church infants received this sacrament immediately after baptism (as they do today in some Eastern rites); and that in the present era children receive it at a tender age. The supernatural is no slave of time. Magdalene and Paul became saints in a split second; and many a person, escaping death by the same timing, rushes to confession and leads a saintly life ever after. We said confirmation "strengthens the supernatural powers," which need time for development by practice.

It is this sacrament that gives prominence to the Person of the Holy Spirit. In instituting it, Christ had in mind the fulfillment of His promise to send the Paraclete. Confirmation is our personal Pentecost. Not with visible fire does He descend into our temple, but with the strength of His love that is vastly more powerful than fire. Of course, as we now know, all Three Divine Persons help in our sanctification (if we cooperate). We call the Holy Spirit the Sanctifier, by "appropriation." We give Him the role of "taking over" where Christ left off (visibly) in establishing His Church. He becomes the fashioner of other Christs, molding the "vessels of clay" from within. This is why the catechism says that in confirmation "the Holy Spirit comes to us in a special way and enables us to profess our faith as strong and perfect Christians and soldiers of Jesus Christ." Accent is on "strong," "perfect," "soldiers."

First, a soldier needs a sense of loyalty to a cause. Confirmation prepares us to accept the Christ-challenge of "commitment," "involvement" in the cause of spreading His Kingdom (Mystical Body); offering Him the use of "another humanity." Next, soldiers need equipment. This the Holy Spirit supplies, as highlighted when the bishop prays the Father to send forth from heaven His sevenfold Spirit, the Holy Paraclete. Hence the Divine Gift-giver, true to His name, enriches not only the powers to believe, trust, and love, but also those baptismal-birthday gifts. These "gifts of the Holy Spirit" enable us to "know" more clearly and to "love" more ardently, giving facility in prayerful language—in fine, to "taste, and see that the Lord is sweet" (Psalms 33:9). As an inducement to use this divine equipment, the Holy Spirit will reward us with the sweetness of His fruits: love, joy, and peace, the radiant decorations of the soldier of Christ.

The essential rite of confirmation shows again the Christo-Trinitarian pattern of the liturgy: "I sign you with the sign of the Cross and I confirm you with the chrism of salvation; in the name of the Father and the Son and the Holy Spirit. Amen."

Baptism and confirmation have intimate relevance to the Eucharist. The first adopts us in Christ, the second matures us in Him, and the Eucharist transforms us in Christ. Thus our approach to Christ through baptism and confirmation is climaxed by personal encounter with Christ Himself hidden under the veils of the Eucharist. There is a twofold direction in the other six sacraments, stemming from the source of the Eucharist, and reception of the same leading back to the Eucharistic goal; "rivulets" with a two-way current—the upward-downward motion of the Mass recurring in the sacramental extension. Baptism and confirmation and the Eucharist have a strong Christ-ward pull.

The Eucharist is the sacrament, par excellence, that keeps alive the extended Incarnation of the Son; His personal Incarnation together with His additional "humanities." As we thus become more thoroughly Christlike by sacramental union, we become more deeply immersed in the bosom of the Father—with Christ, "knowing" the Father more intimately; with Christ and the Holy Spirit, "loving" the Father more intensely. The union wrought by Holy Communion so transforms us in Christ that, without exaggeration, but as a factual experience, we say with St. Paul: "It is now no longer I that live, but Christ lives in me" (Galatians 2:20)—no longer I that pray, but Christ *prays* in me.

We shall never achieve perfect "active participation" until every member offering Christ in the Mass receives Him back in Communion. The whole Mass is a two-way prayer, and faith is a substitute for 20/20 vision, not 20/40. The most tragic lines ever penned are: "He came unto his own, and his own received him not" (John 1:11). The tragedy reverberates even to this Eucharistic "age."

Penance, matrimony, and holy orders relate to the Eucharist more as consequences than as leads; solidifying our transformation and deepening it.

Penance is divinely medicinal, curative, and preventative, thus restoring and strengthening transformation.

Matrimony is always marriage *in Christ*, and designed for fruitful extension of His Mystical Body with its future members.

Holy orders extend Christ's priestly office and assure the continuity of the sacramental current, especially the Eucharist.

Extreme unction prepares the temple for release of the soul, identified with Christ, for its journey toward the vision, there to be face to face with God, within the divine bosom of the Father, in the embrace of Triune blissful Love.

Throughout the conferring of these sacraments we see the abiding presence of the Three Divine Persons, and Their names announced repeatedly. The same is true of the numberless blessings for the sacramentals that graciously fill this world, among persons, places, and things, and the "fragrance of Christ for God" (2 Corinthians 2:15).

If the Eucharist is a center, its radius is more embracing than we generally realize. On one horizon it reaches the Liturgy of heaven. Our connection with angelic choirs in the Sanctus is no forced flight of fancy. For there is only one sacrifice, one official offerer, one Victim—Christ. Christ on His heavenly throne, in glory at the right of the Father, is the same Christ of the altar, and the Christ of the soul, within each temple.

Do not the sacramental words of the Mass, almost immediately after the Consecration, unveil a vista of the Liturgy of heaven when we ask the Father: "Most humbly we implore Thee, almighty God, bid these our mystic offerings to be brought by the hands of Thy holy Angel unto Thy altar above, before the face of Thy divine majesty; that those of us who, by sharing in the Sacrifice of this altar, *shall receive* the most sacred Body and Blood of Thy Son, may be filled with every grace and heavenly blessing. Through the same Christ our Lord. Amen."

St. Paul delineates for us this heavenly aspect of the Mass: "For Jesus has not entered into a Holies made by hands, a mere copy of the true, but into heaven itself, to appear now before the face of God on our behalf"

(Hebrews 9:24). St. John envisioned the same: "And I saw, and behold, in the midst of the throne...a Lamb standing, as if slain" (Apocalypse 5:6).

The sacrifice offered to the Father on behalf of men, then, has eternal consequences. The same sacrifice of atonement, adoration, thanksgiving, and supplication offered on the Cross is simultaneously perpetuated sacramentally in the Mass on earth and in the state of glory in heaven; offered corporately with His Mystical Body under each condition, by the members of the Church Militant and the Church Triumphant. When time shall be no more and there will remain only the triumphant Church, Christ with His Mystical Body will eternally offer the sacrifice of adoration, love, and thanksgiving. We shall concelebrate one sublime High Mass—the highest ever!

The opposite horizon of the Mass is terrestrial. The *Ite Missa Est* does not mean: Go, the Mass is ended. For the Mass will never end. These words convey a commission: Go forth. You are dismissed to carry the fruits of the Mass into the wide world; into the home, the marketplace, the office, the playground. You are Christ-bearers, salt of the earth, light of the world.

But the fruits of the Mass depend on the intensity put into the offering. What would help to increase the fervor of our offering is to realize that we live in a Mass atmosphere. The most dynamic activity occurring in this world is the Mass, which necessarily becomes the world's center. Around the clock, "from the rising of the sun even to the going down, my name is great among the

Gentiles, and in every place there is sacrifice, and there is offered to my name a clean oblation" (Mal. 1:11).

Surely this should make us Mass-conscious. Perhaps we can learn from Sister Elizabeth of the Trinity how she joined liturgical with personal prayer.

Shortly before she died she wrote out the inspirations of her "last retreat," which she entitled "A Praise of Glory," the adopted name she gave herself, for she wanted to live and die as a praise of glory to the Trinity. It was St. Paul who gave her this idea: "Blessed be the God and Father of our Lord Jesus Christ, who has blessed us with every spiritual blessing on high in Christ. Even as he chose us in him before the foundation of the world, that we should be holy and without blemish in his sight in love. He predestined us to be adopted through Jesus Christ as his sons, according to the purpose of his will, unto the *praise of the glory* of his grace, with which he has favored us in his beloved Son" (Ephesians 1:3–5).

On the fourteenth day of her retreat Sister Elizabeth wrote: "The Apostle has often revealed the grandeur of this vocation: God chose us...that we may be unto the praise of His glory. How can we respond to the dignity of our vocation? This is the secret, 'I live, now not I, but Christ lives in me.'...Hence I must study this divine Model, so thoroughly identifying myself with Him that I can incessantly show Him forth to His Father."[6]

By this last expression, to "incessantly show Him forth to His Father," she means that she took the "Accept, most holy Trinity, this offering" from the context of the Missal and incorporated it in her prayer within the dwelling of her soul. It is in the temple that the Mass ends its earthly horizon.

From all this we see that the Offering of the Mass has three theaters: altar, throne, temple.

## *Notes*

1.      *Summa, III*, Q. 65, Art. 3.
2.      *Mediator Dei*, Nos. 23, 24.
3.      *Ibid.*, Nos. 28, 29, 30.
4.      *Ibid.*, No. 14.
5.      *Catechism of the Council of Trent*, Part II, Chap. 4, n. 47.
6.      Marie-Michel Philipon, O.P., ed., *The Spiritual Doctrine of Sister Elizabeth of the Trinity* (Westminster, Md.: Newman Press, 1947), p. 251.

# FOURTEEN

# *Family Spirit*

"The family that prays together, stays together." This is because prayer is a bond that unites such a family to God, and God is Love. It is impossible to be truly in contact with the fire of God's love without radiating its warmth to others. That is to say, if one really loves God he must reflect this love to all with whom he comes in contact. This is true for two reasons. First, it follows from the law by which love operates, a sort of spiritual law of gravity; flowing from the Head to one member it continues (if not hindered) to influence other members in the Mystical Body, like blood from the heart coursing through several arteries. Secondly, Christ formulated a law that we must activate: "That you love one another as I have loved you" (John 15:12).

This we have already previewed when describing prayer as the language of the soul which expresses our love for God and which requires that we prove our love for God by loving our neighbor. The first "neighbors" we come in contact with are the members of our own family. All families were created to "stay together," and love, generated by prayer, provides the bond.

An individual family bound by love simply follows the pattern of the Divine Family: Father and Son united by Their breathing bond of Love, the Holy Spirit. But according to the plan, divine adoption has incorporated us into the Mystical Body of Christ, Who incorporates us into the intimacy of the divine bosom. We suddenly realize, then, that our neighbors have multiplied fabulously; that, in fact, we have joined an immense throng who make up the Family of God; and, finally, that truly to belong to this Family demands that we love all its members.

Thus a praying family, individual or corporate, keeps together by the Spirit of Love, Who is a "Holy Spirit" or the "Family Spirit." We have no clearer illustration than the Mass, the family prayer par excellence. Not only do we here see the Divine Family prominent by Their very names, but we also see the many members of the Mystical Body closely knit by the Family Spirit. Most of the prayers incorporated in the Mass are in the plural: Let us pray; the Lord be with you; we beseech Thee; have mercy on us; my sacrifice and yours; Our Father, etc. There are also the mementoes in which we "remember" in our praying the pope and bishop; all those present; the saints; the faithful departed. We include every member on earth, in heaven, in purgatory.

Never do we see the family spirit more evident than at the family meal. Think of the work, sacrifice, and love put into its preparation—all for the purpose of sharing the happy result in a little family feast (whether of stew or steak); all relaxed, as they are nourished as well as united by the same food.

But what of the divine banquet of the Mass? The very symbolism of the bread and wine points up the classic example of unity obtained in Holy Communion. As each loaf of bread contains so many particles of wheat, and the wine comes from the juice of so many grapes, all communicants become so many "particles" fused more intimately together by the family spirit. This becomes evident as we see kneeling side by side people of all kinds and ages: the child of eight and the genius of eighty; the rich man and the poor man; the European, the African, the American, the Asiatic.

Nor is the supper idea missing. Every Communion table is but an extended leaf of the Lord's Table used at the Last Supper where He fed several from *one* loaf of the Consecrated Bread; where He shared with several *one* chalice of Wine—His Flesh and Blood which, then as now, are the life of the world, life uniting the world. " 'And the bread that I will give is my flesh for the life of the world.... Amen, amen, I say to you, unless you eat the flesh of the Son of Man, and drink his blood, you shall not have life in you'" (John 6:52, 54). "O Lord Jesus Christ, Son of the living God, who according to the will of Thy Father, through the cooperation of the Holy Spirit, hast given life to the world: deliver me by this Thy most holy Body and Blood from all my transgressions and from every evil; make me always adhere to Thy commandments" (first Communion prayer in the Mass).

As we said, Christ accomplished His most significant "business" in the prayer He offered on the Cross to redeem all men. This prayer-action He continues in the mass. And it is in the Mass that we, in family fashion, join Him. It is likewise from the Mass that we take our cue of carrying over the family spirit into our daily contacts, helping all the redeemed to save themselves. This again recalls the commission of the *Ite Missa Est*.

Since the Incarnation, Christ is the center of this world. He is the focal point of history, past, present, future. These divisions of time merge and become mere facets in the external central act of Calvary, which remains eternally present in the Mass. The keen, penetrating observation uttered by Ambassador Birel, a non-Catholic, as an explanation for the spiritual strength of Ireland in contrast to England, "It is the Mass that matters," conveys a deeper impact than a mere comparison. The phrase, now a frequent slogan, also shows the Mass as a "school" or pattern for Christian living. In other words, it is the Mass that matters because we are to "live the Mass."

We learn to live by living. Hence it is easy to learn the art of Christian living from the Mass because it is so vital an action. Once we see the social import, especially of the Communion and the *Ite*, we know what to do. It becomes all the easier when we realize that we live the Mass *with* Christ. But, of course, in living the Mass, we must not forget all He taught us before He gave us the Mass.

We recall that He referred to Himself as the way, the truth, the life. Christ loved to simplify, we love to complicate. By that I mean Our Lord synthesized His entire Gospel message by teaching the truth that He was the way leading to the Father, and giving us His life so that we could follow His path. There is only one Christ Who is at the same time the way, truth, life. This is what the first followers of Christ saw in the gospel, their only "textbook."

Lacking this simplicity, we now have theology: dogmatic, moral, sacramental, ascetical, mystical, liturgical; or, if you prefer, the creed, commandments, sacraments. We think if we know our theology or our catechism, we know Christ. This does not follow. The man who gives a generous contribution on Sunday and resorts to deceit on Monday does not see Christ in the seventh commandment. The woman who receives Communion and, with the same tongue, is uncharitable to her neighbor on the way home does not see Christ in the eighth commandment.

The trouble is that we love to departmentalize too much. We miss the whole for the parts; the whole Christ for the catechism questions, or divisions of theology. Pius Parsch puts it well: "It is not theologically accurate to place the full essence of Christian life in upright, moral living, doing good and avoiding evil. Morality is not the ultimate. The essence of the Christian life is the kingdom of God, supernatural grace. Morality is a necessary sequel. Since we are privileged to have God living in our hearts and to have His kingdom developing within us, it follows that we must live virtuously. How nobly we would live, if we were convinced of bearing God's kingdom within us."[1]

The Christian life does not consist in keeping the commandments or in practicing the virtues, but rather in appreciating and living the Christ-Life within our souls. Aware of such a priceless privilege, naturally we refrain from sin and instinctively perform the works of charity.

Just as the "proper study of mankind is man," the proper study of Christianity is Christ. The subject matter of all theology is Christ, Who tried to clarify this fact by His triple title, way-truth-life. Before giving us the very social action of the Mass, He conditioned us by showing us the social aspect of the commandments, the Creed, and the other sacraments. This we too often miss. We need to recall it, in order to strengthen the family spirit. You see, the Son came as Representative of the Family to seek more members. His greatest truth was the secret of the Trinity, containing within it all other truths. As these unfold, they reflect the same social aspect.

We have seen the gigantic scope of the doctrine of the creation of the universe. In retrospect we can recall the happy alliance between angelic, human, and material worlds. What a social atmosphere this makes for all God's creatures!

We saw, too, the solidarity of our race in the Incarnation, which brought forth the King of the universe. Linked to this is the doctrine of original sin, the immediate occasion of the Incarnation. The story of the fall only intensifies our oneness. By the sin of the first Adam the entire human race fell, and the price of the redemption, paid by the second Adam, repurchased every single son of the first, without exception. "I, if I be lifted up from the earth, will draw all things to myself" (John 12:32). Christ said to Simon, "Upon this rock I will build my Church"—not churches, but *one* for all. The same Church would have one protector: "But the Advocate, the Holy Spirit, whom the Father will send in my name, he will teach you all things, and bring to your mind all that I have said to you" (John 14:26). This one Church we see linked to the Church Triumphant and the Church Suffering in the Communion of Saints, uniting three worlds in Christ. And how very sociable the final assignment: "Go, therefore, and make disciples of all nations" (Matthew 28:19).

For knitting all these truths closer to the Teacher, as well as knitting disciple closer to disciple, we have only to recall why He came to teach: "God is love" (1 John 4:8); "For God so loved the world that he gave his only-begotten Son" (John 3:16). In Christ, the Truth, then, we are all linked together by love. This is not over-simplifying, but only getting back to the simplicity of Christ.

This love should be manifest in our every act, in both intention and execution. We have already seen the social character of the Eucharist in the family praying and eating together. And just as all the other sacraments relate to the Eucharist, so they share in its social nature. Too often we think of them in the first person: "I have to get my baby baptized. I am going to confession. I made my confirmation. I am going to be married. I was anointed. My son was ordained."

We must recall the grandeur of the liturgy; the inner grandeur beneath the simplicity of bread, wine, water, oil; beneath the richness of ceremony. We must remember that the sacraments make the Mystical Body of Christ more vibrant and glorious; extending its influence. Then our thinking would be more social. We would hear something like this:

> My child is going to be adopted today. He will be another light for the world, somebody to set it on fire for love of Christ; salt of the earth to give it flavor and a thirst for Christ.
>
> I am going to confess my sins because every sin causes tremendous upheavals of worldwide repercussions in the divine plan for a one-family world. All the members of Christ's Body have been weakened by my personal offenses.
>
> I have received the sacrament which confirmed the Christ-Life within me and enabled me to fulfill my vocation to spread the kingdom of God in the world.
>
> We are going to be united in marriage with Christ, to sanctify our love which we hope will be made fruitful with other Christs to people heaven and earth.
>
> I received the sacrament of the sick which strengthened my soul when I was seriously

ill, which sealed my sense through which I had sinned and prepared my soul for a safe release; but the healing of my soul carried over to restore my body to health, that I may continue to spread Christ through the world.

I gave my son to God that he may be another Christ, enabling Him to extend His priesthood so that millions more may adore the Father, to baptize, absolve, anoint, preach, console, and direct thousands to become splendid temples of God for time and eternity.

All this would bespeak the love in our hearts for God and for each other.

Many people qualify their acceptance of the commandments and like to see how far they can go without committing a mortal sin. Sometimes moral theologians write tomes on the subject. But Christ simplified the commandments also. Here again He used the magic formula: love. And, of course, since it is the same Image of Love Who reflects the way as He does the truth, we must look for the same social content in the commandments. This really bothers us. It is easy to live sociably with doctrines and sacraments, but with people—all people—that can be hard. For this reason Christ gave us His Life, and before the *Ite* there is always the meal with Divine Bread.

In the first place, Christ showed us the fallacy of trying to love God while despising our neighbor: "'Two went up to the temple to pray, the one a Pharisee and the other a publican. The Pharisee stood and began to pray thus within himself: "O God, I thank thee that I am not like the rest of men, robbers, dishonest, adulterers, or even like this publican. I fast twice a week; I pay tithes of al that I possess." But the publican, standing afar off, would not so much as lift up his eyes to heaven, but kept striking his breast, saying, "O God, be merciful to me a sinner!" I tell you that this man went back to his home justified rather than the other; for everyone who exalts himself shall be humbled, and he who humbles himself shall be exalted'" (Luke 18:10–14).

Many people in the time of Christ did not know who were their neighbors, as frequently happens today. "And behold, a certain lawyer got up to test him, saying "Master, what must I do to gain eternal life?' But he said to him, 'What is written in the Law? How dost thou read?' He answered and said, *Thou shalt love the Lord thy God with thy whole heart, and with thy whole soul, and with thy whole strength, and with thy whole mind; and thy neighbor as thyself.* And he said to him, 'Thou has answered rightly; do this and thou shalt live.' But he, wishing to justify himself, said to Jesus, 'And who is my neighbor?'" (Luke 10:25–29). In response, Jesus gave one of His most brilliant story-lessons, the parable of the Good Samaritan. It stunned his hearers. The status of one's neighbor became settled for all time. For if a Samaritan was neighborly to a Jew, and a Jew had to "go and do likewise," then everyone is neighbor to everyone else.

To eliminate any ifs, ands, or buts on this question, Christ on another question said: "But I say to you, love your *enemies*, do good to those who hate you, and pray for those who persecute and calumniate you, so that you may be the children of your Father in heaven, who makes his sun to rise on the good and evil, and sends rain on the just and unjust. For if you love those who love you, what reward shall you have? Do not even the publicans do that? And if you salute your brethren only, what are you doing more than others? Do not even the Gentiles do that? You therefore are to be perfect, even as your heavenly Father is perfect" (Matthew 5:44–48).

At another time when a doctor of the law asked which was the greatest commandment, Christ said: *"Thou shalt love the Lord thy God with thy whole heart, and with thy whole soul, and with thy whole mind.* This is the greatest and first commandment. And the second is like it, *Thou shalt love thy neighbor as thyself.* On these two commandments depend the whole Law and the Prophets" (Matthew 22:37–40). This shows us plainly that the "whole Law" of the Ten Commandments is shot through with love. But why ten, if two contain it all? The first three refer to God, the others to our neighbor. The last seven detail specific circumstances under which we meet our neighbor, from day to day; detailed so that we will make no mistakes in not loving him on all occasions: loving reverence for the authority of our parents and superiors, for the life, honor, property and reputation of our neighbor.

With recurring emphasis, as if turning a golden coin round and round, Christ stressed His twofold law of love. Touching are the final echoes of this message heard as the Last Supper ended, after Mass: "Little children, yet a little while I am with you.... A new commandment I give you that you love one another: that as I have loved you, you also love one another. By this will all men know that you are my disciples, if you have love for one another" (John 13:33–35). Reference to a "new commandment" meant that the "old" statutes now took on a new meaning and life, baptized so to speak in the reflection of the Image: "as I have loved you," because I have loved you, in the measure with which I have loved you.

Like the symphony it is, the last discourse repeats the same theme at intervals, as follows: "If you love me, keep my commandments.... If anyone love me, he will keep my word.... If you keep my commandments you will abide in my love.... This is my commandment, that you love one another as I have loved you.... These things I command you, that you may love one another" (John 14:15, 23; 15:10, 12, 17). And in this same discourse Christ simplified our program for following Him, as "the way, and the truth, and the life" (John 14:6).

It was the pen of John that recorded this symphony of love. He saved the fiery, forceful eloquence of his commentary for his First Epistle.

> I write of what was from the beginning, what we have heard, what we have seen with our eyes, what we have looked upon and our hands have handled: of the Word of Life. And the Life was made known and we have seen, and now testify and announce to you, the Life Eternal which was with the Father, and has appeared to us. What we have seen and heard

we announce to you, in order that you also may have fellowship with us, and that our fellowship may be with the Father and with his Son Jesus Christ.... If we say that we have fellowship with him, and walk in darkness, we lie and are not practicing the truth. But if we walk in the light as he also is in the light, we have fellowship with one another (1 John 1:1–3, 6–7).

And by this we can be sure that we know him, if we keep his commandments. He who says that he knows him and does not keep his commandments, is a liar and the truth is not in him.... He who says that he is in the light and hates his brother, is in the darkness still. He who loves his brother abides in the light, and for him there is no stumbling. But he who hates his brother is in the darkness, and walks in the darkness, and does not know whither he goes; because the darkness has blinded his eyes.... Everyone who hates his brother is a murderer. And you know that no murderer has eternal life abiding in him (1 John 2:3–4, 9–11; 3:15).

Beloved, let us love one another, for love is from God. And everyone who loves is born of God, and knows God.... In this has the love of God been shown in our case, that God has sent His only-begotten Son into the world that we may live through him.... Beloved, if God has so loved us, we also ought to love one another (1 John 4:7, 9, 11).

It is precisely because of the "new look" that Christ gave to love of neighbor that the spiritual and corporal works of mercy introduce the chapters on the commandments in the catechism. These serve to particularize, even more, the seven laws for loving our neighbor. Here we find the core of Christian social service: aiding the hungry, thirsty, naked, imprisoned, homeless, sick, dead, sinful, ignorant, worried, sorrowful, inimical. For those who think we can "take this or leave it" there is a warning: there will come a day of the great division. The sheep will hear a positive decision; the goats, a negative one. "For I was hungry and you gave me to eat; I was thirsty and you have me to drink; I was a stranger and you took me in; naked and you covered me; sick and you visited me; I was in prison and you came to me" (Matthew 25:35–36).

When we lose our way on a trip by getting sidetracked on the wrong road, the way back seems endless, as we circle around. But once we stop for a map we are all set. Maps are so clear, so simple. They give us the plan of our trip. Christ gave us a plan, a simple plan, a family plan. Yet the world has lost its way. The solution? Back to the plan: the true way of life. You can do something about it. Remember you were confirmed to commitment. The tragic Hamlet surely had it hard when he said: "The time is out of joint: O cursed spite, that ever I was born to set it right!" Well might we echo his first statement, but stress the positive element in the second: O blessed grace that I was born to set it right!

In the first place, we have to see how the plan got lost; how liars sowed lies. We have seen the pattern of the Divine Family throughout the universe; now in a shadow, now in trace, now in image. In the Mystical Body the Image breathes with life of a spirit. Patterns can fade with time, but we can always restore patterns. So when we recognize loose threads of the pattern of the Mystical Body for the loose threads that they are, we take the first steps toward restoring them. Moreover, the less loose threads there are, the more integral the pattern remains.

What are these dangling, untidy fringes seen today? Rugged individualism, antisocial attitudes, isolationism, racism, statism, commercialism, vandalism, atheism (abstractions for concrete realities). All these do not and cannot make sense, because they lie outside a plan that is eternal and divine. They all reveal the focal point of today's worldwide epidemic, social schizophrenia, which is basically not so much a splitting of individual personalities, of segments within nations, of nation from nation, as a splitting of the Trinitarian pattern extended in the masterpiece of the created universe.

Hanging by threads is precarious and dangerous to those involved. Loose threads must be sewed back or perish. This is why fear should give way to hope. We really have no need to fear enemies who have no ground on which to stand. Our need is to clear the atmosphere and fix our gaze on the Center, Who has given us fixed horizons. What we need is just another revolution. We are, of course, recommending, for a change of pace, a peaceful revolution; a revolving back where we evolved from—the *esprit de corps* of the early Christians, to whom the pagans pointed saying "See the Christians, how they love one another!" Impossible, impractical? By no means.

In fact, the revolution has already started, with many steps in the right direction: United Nations, Peace Corps, exchange students, adoption of refugee children, integration, profit-sharing, lay missionaries, Christian Family Movement, Christophers, Legion of Mary, Ecumenism. Volunteers are need to push the Christ-ward movement. But there is a string attached to the volunteer element. We are not free to refuse at least to pray for the cause; not free if we wish to live divinely. All life must follow life, or die. The law of Divine Life is the law of love. For those who bristle in the face of all laws, we have only to substitute the softer terms: Christian togetherness, *esprit de corps*, Family Spirit.

We can do no better than to close this chapter as Christ closed His last message—with prayer. His prayer: "Holy Father, keep in thy name those thou hast given me, that they may be one even as we are.... Yet not for these only do I pray, but for those also who through their word are to believe in me, that all may be one, even as thou, Father, in me and I in thee; that they also may be one in us, that the world may believe that thou hast sent me.... And I have made known to them thy name, and will make it known, in order that the love with which thou hast loved me may be in them, and I in them" (John 17:11, 20–21, 26).

After sealing His message of love with prayer, He proceeded to seal it with blood, sprinkled immediately afterwards in the Garden, showered the next day from the tree—offered and received each day in the Mass.

## *Notes*

1.      *Church's Year of Grace*, tr. D. F. Coogan, Jr., and R. Kraus (Collegeville, Minn.: Liturgical Press, St. John's Abbey, 1953). Vol. I, pp. 95–96.

# FIFTEEN

## *Family Reunion*

One thing that bothers us from time to time is the fact that, wonderful though the secrets of the supernatural are, we cannot see them. They are so intangible. True, but one day we shall see them, provided we hold on. Faith is the handle we hold. Faith is a gift, of course, but surprisingly enough, considering its priceless value, it is for free. It is ours for the asking—the more we ask, the more we receive. When the blind man prayed, "O Lord, that I may see," he saw not only outwardly but also inwardly.

The lift we need, while holding on, is courage. St. Paul knew. "Always full of courage, then, and knowing that while we are in the body we are exiled from the Lord—for we walk by faith and not by sight" (2 Corinthians 5:6–7). And St. John goads on our courage by promising us "sight": "Beloved, now we are the children of God, and it is not yet appeared what we shall be. We know that, when he appears, we shall be like to him, for we shall see him just as he is" (1 John 3:2).

Death for a pagan is the saddest thing in the world. Death for a Christian is the most joyous thing in the world. For a pagan, life ends at death. For a Christian, life begins, not at forty or fifty, but at death. For the Christian, death is the gateway to life, to another world vastly more intriguing than Mars and all other such planets. Sometimes there is an intermediary world, a blessed world of waiting; sometimes there is a nonstop flight to the world of heaven.

But heaven is such a mysterious place (it *is* a place), we do not know anything about it! Oh, but we do! The mystery element makes it all the more full of wonder and enticement. To those who look forward to visiting the Grand Canyon or Yellowstone National Park, it is mystery that lures them on. No pictures completely capture mystery. It must be seen. And so it is with heaven. There we shall have the vision of the Divine Family, gazing at Them face to face in the home They made for us.

Never was it truer than in this connection, that "there is no place like home." The fact is, though we do not realize it, we have a tremendous tug toward this home where there will be a grand Family reunion. The enormous craving for happiness in every human heart, never satisfied, is a symptom of deep-seated nostalgia for heaven. It is not only a supernatural longing, but fundamentally natural. It is congenital. St. Augustine put his finger on it. He ought to know, for he surely tried every means of attaining happiness. But he said, "Our hearts are made for Thee, O God, and they are restless until they rest in Thee."

Earth, at best, is exile and separation. We are cut off from the Vision of God, walking "by faith and not by sight," and it has not yet appeared "what we shall be." Heaven will unite us by sight, "face to face we shall see God." The promise, "We will come to him and make our abode with him," will be gloriously fulfilled. There will no longer be need for the sublime words of the Son, nor those of the Spirit breathed through John and Paul. We shall see the Word, reflecting the light of the Father in the warmth of Their Love. Theologians use the term "light of glory" to describe the added power that the Trinity gives our minds in heaven, enabling us to become united to Them in this face-to-face vision. The "light of light" we mention in the Credo will reflect itself in our souls.

Sometimes people wonder what we shall do in heaven. In the first place, we shall be so happy that we could not be any happier. We shall enjoy perfect fulfillment of the happiness we were made for. We shall experience perfect repose and the most exhilarating activity at the same time. How? That is part of the mystery awaiting us. There will be nothing impersonal in all this joy. On the contrary, each of us will enter into the closest possible intimacy with the Divine Persons. Not till then will we understand what it is to "know" and "love." We will not know the Truth but recognize It; we will not yearn to embrace Love but will possess It.

According to the nature of love, in heaven this intimate love will be reciprocal. "Behold, I stand at the door and knock. If any man listens to my voice and opens the door to me, I will come in to him and will sup with him, and he with me. He who overcomes, I will permit him to sit with me upon my throne; as I also have overcome and have sat with my Father on his throne" (Apocalypse 3:20–21). The atmosphere will be ever joyous. "And God will wipe away every tear from their eyes. And death shall be no more; neither shall there be mourning, no crying, nor pain any more, for the former things have passed away" (Apocalypse 21:4).

At the end of the world, the bodies we left behind will join us again. But what a difference! No more of that tired feeling, nor gray hairs, no colds or sunburns, no more outside make-up nor inside surgery, and no more dying. Our resurrected bodies will be glorified, full of luminosity, clarity, brilliant beauty. We shall outshine the stars. The *lumen goriae* of our soul will diffuse itself and break through to the body. We shall be able to travel from place to place with the speed of light.

Sometimes we might envy the apostles and disciples who lived in the close company of Christ, the people He comforted and the children He blessed. What we missed we shall find in heaven. His voice will bring His words to our ears; His face will smile as He looks into our eyes. Waiting nearly two thousand years to preside at this reunion is our Blessed Mother, who will welcome us in heaven. We shall see her, talk to her, thank her. We shall see our guardian angel, and in case we did not appreciate his services on earth there will be an eternity to make up for this, as he will be our constant companion in heaven. To the saints to whom we prayed again their intercession we can render thanks. We shall get to know those souls whom we may have aided in seeking "perpetual light."

Last but not least, there will be the warmest reunion with our beloved relatives and friends. We know the happy anticipation there is in reunions on earth: meeting former classmates and recalling days full of happy memories; gathering of kith and kin that are gladdened by the "old familiar faces." Such experiences are sunbeams reflecting the shining happiness of the heavenly homeland. "Then the just will shine forth like the sun in the kingdom of their Father" (Matthew 13:43). Glorification will not lessen the tenderness of our love for our own, but rather increase it, as the *lumen gloriae* shines through, from God, to us, to them. And there will be so much to talk about!

What is more, the beauty we loved in this world we shall continue to enjoy. How very much at home we shall really be! God promised us this taking up of the world and glorifying it in heaven way back in the days of the prophets. Peter recalled it in one of his letters: "But we look for new heavens and a new earth, according to his promises" (2 Peter 3:13).

It is to His beloved disciple that Christ revealed this in the clearest terms. He gave John a preview of heaven which he records in the Apocalypse, the last book of the New Testament. "And I saw a new heaven and a new earth.... And he who was sitting on the throne said, 'Behold I make all things new!' And he said, 'Write, for these words are trustworthy and true'" (Apocalypse 21:1, 5).

The vision depicts heaven as a magnificent city:

> But the city itself is pure gold, like pure glass. And the foundations of the wall of the city were adorned with every precious stone.... And the twelve gates were twelve pearls; that is, each gate was of a single pearl. And the street of the city was pure gold, as it were transparent glass.... And the city has no need of the sun or the moon to shine upon it. For the glory of God lights it up, and the Lamb is the lamp thereof. And the nations shall walk by the light thereof; and the kings of the earth shall bring their glory and honor into it. And its gates shall not be shut by day; for there shall be no night there (Apocalypse 21:18–19, 21, 23–25).

What does all this mean? It is but a preview, vivid in oriental imagery, of the "new heaven" that the Trinity will refashion, as the earthly habitation into which the Incarnate Son entered in becoming flesh, and which contributed to the making of the human race, becomes supernaturalized amid all the splendors of heaven. But rich metaphors can never capture the mystery of it all, even though couched in inspired words. *"Eye has not seen nor ear heard, nor has it entered into the heart of man, what things God has prepared for those who love him"* (1 Corinthians 2:9).

In short, in heaven the Communion of Saints will merge into a union of saints, all moved into the home of the Father, with the Family of God—where the secret will be secret no longer.

The story of the Divine Family you already know. You know it by heart. In condensed form you recite it each day in the Creed, from beginning to end. The first part tells of the secret; the second of its meaning for you.

I believe in God, the *Father* Almighty, *Creator* of *heaven* and *earth*; and in *Jesus Christ*, His only *Son,* our Lord; who was conceived by the Holy Spirit, born of the *Virgin Mary*,...was *crucified, died,* and was buried;...the third day he rose again from the dead; He *ascended* into heaven.... I believe in the *Holy Spirit*, the Holy Catholic Church [adoption, indwelling, Mystical Body], the *Communion of Saints* [brotherly love], the forgiveness of sins [preservation and reinstatement], the resurrection of the body [reunion], and the life everlasting [vision, face to face].

# Index